KEEP GETTING BETTER: AT LEARNING

Gerry Corrigan

Copyright © 2025 (Gerry Corrigan)
All rights reserved worldwide.

No part of the book may be copied or changed in any format, sold, or used in a way other than what is outlined in this book, under any circumstances, without the prior written permission of the publisher.

Inspiring Publishers
P.O. Box 159, Calwell, ACT Australia 2905
Email: publishaspg@gmail.com
http://www.inspiringpublishers.com

Cover artwork by giraffe.com.au. Illustration by Nicholas Castro.

 A catalogue record for this book is available from the National Library of Australia

National Library of Australia The Prepublication Data Service

Author: Gerry Corrigan
Title: Keep Getting Better: at Learning
Genre: Non-fiction

Paperback ISBN: 978-1-923250-80-2
eBook ISBN: 978-1-923250-81-9
ePub2 ISBN: 978-1-923250-82-6

Table of Contents

List of figures vii
Chapter One: Introduction 1
   Foreword 1
   Why is this book important? 3
   Using learning process maps to explore how learners learn 8
   Decision-making—a different perspective 9
   Getting better at learning 11
   Learning process analysis to generate feedback 12
   Using microanalysis as a basis for feedback 12
   The business of learning 13
   Learning as a purposeful activity 13
   It's not about decision-making—it's about learning 15
   How do we get better at learning? 16
   An example of learning process analysis in action .. 17
   The value proposition of learning process analysis .. 19
Chapter Two: Learning process maps and how they work 24
   What is a learning process map? 24
   The components of a learning process map 24
   How do you 'read' a learning process map? 25
   Making sense of a learning process map 27
   Categorising learners' decisions and their reasons
for their decisions 27
   Constructing a learning process map 31
      Step 1: to extract learners' decisions 31
      Step 2: to extract learners' decisions 31

    Step 3: constructing the learning process map 35
    Step 4: categorising the decisions and reasons
    in a learning process map 37
Chapter Three: Learning process analysis for learning 38
    What learning process analysis can do 38
    Increasing the visibility of learning 39
    Variability in learning outcomes 40
Chapter Four: The underlying principles of learning
process analysis 44
    Principle 1 44
    Principle 2 44
    Categories of decisions 45
    Decisions result in other decisions 45
    Decisions are underpinned by reasons 47
    Problem Based Learning 49
    The principles of learning process analysis and PBL 50
    The importance of the two principles of learning
    process analysis 55
    Learners will have different reasons for the same decision
    (a case study) 58
    In summary—decisions are made for reasons, always 65
Chapter Five: Insights from research that inform
learning process analysis 66
    Research insights into learning process analysis 66
    The precise nature of learners' decision-making
    can be extracted, mapped and categorised 67
    Insights into decision-making about learning 68
    Feedback to learners about their decision-making
    can assist in achieving improved learning outcomes. 70
Chapter Six: Using learning process maps to get better 71
    Introduction 71
    As a feedback tool 73
    Learning process analysis and knowledge acquisition 74
    Self-regulated and self-directed learning 76
    Soft-skill detection 78

Chapter Seven: Real world applications of learning
process analysis 79
   Soft skills in the workplace 79
   Mapping to assess soft skill use 81
   Mapping group collaboration 81
   The utility of understanding collaboration 88
   Collaboration for self-regulated learning 89
   Mapping creativity and learning 91
   Mapping critical thinking/clinical reasoning 93
   Small group work 94
   Social constructivism 100
   The practical use 101
   Learning about problem solving 103

Chapter Eight: How to use learning process maps
to help learners 105
   Introduction 105
   Using video to capture decision-making 106
   Using proforma data capture 112
   Stimulated Recall Interviewing 115
   Some practice exercises—constructing learning
   process maps 119
   Constructing maps 121
      Constructing a learning process map—
      from video data 122
      Constructing a learning process map—
      from proforma data 125
      Assigning categories of decisions and reasons 126
      Decision categories: 128
      Descriptions of each category 129
   Analysing learning process maps 130
      Analysing maps for individuals 132
      Tracking the development of soft skills 134
   Learning process analysis is a descriptive method 135
   Appendix 8.1: proforma example 1 136

Appendix 8.2: proforma example 2 143
Appendix 8.3: solutions to worked examples 145
Chapter Nine: Where to from here? 147
   Learning process analysis and learning—
   and you and your learners 147
   Deploying learning process analysis in corporate
   and governance scenarios 148
   Mapping as a potential decision-making audit tool 149
   Diagnosing inconsistency in decision-making 152
Chapter Ten: Learning process analysis as a research tool 156
   Learning process analysis to measure governance
   and management 157
   Learning process analysis and artificial intelligence 159
   Future possibilities 161

List of figures

Figure 1.1: An example of a decision with reasoning of the student 6
Figure 1.2: An example of a learning process map (decision + reason/s) 8
*Figure 1.3: Learning process map of Stephen in a
problem-based learning (PBL) tutorial 14*
Figure 1.4: LPA and how it works 15
Figure 1.5: Learning process map for a student in a small-group tutorial.... 18
Figure 2.1: Learning process map showing sequential direction 25
Figure 2.2: Learning process map showing sequential direction 26
Figure 2.3a: Taxonomic divisions in LPA 29
Figure 2.3b: Taxonomic divisions in LPA 30
Figure 2.3c: Taxonomic divisions in LPA 30
Figure 2.4: The steps required to construct a learning process map 32
Figure 2.5: A students returned proforma (reconstructed) 33
*Figure 2.6: A learning process map developed from the above proforma
and interview 37*
Figure 3.1: Learning process map for a grade 6 visual arts student 41
*Figure 3.2: Learning process map for a post-graduate medical student
in a problem-based learning tutorial 42*
Figure 4.1: Decisions as prerequisites 46
Figure 4.2: Learning process map showing decisions and reasons why 48
Figure 4.3: The role that learning process analysis can play 49
*Figure 4.4: Learning process map of a student for session 1 (out of 3)
in a medical problem-based learning session 51*
Figure 4.5: Highlighting part of the value of learning process analysis 52
Figure 4.6: For learner C in a PBL session 53
Figure 4.7: Decision-making in session 2 of a PBL problem 54
*Figure 4.8: Learning process map of a student undertaking
an art project 56*
Figure 4.9a and 4.9b: Different reasons for the same decision 60

Figure 4.9c 61
Figure 4.9d 62
Figure 4.9e 63
Figure 4.9f 64
Figure 4.9g 64
Figure 5.1: The three main methods for extracting learners' decisions
and reasons 67
Figure 5.2: Revealing the implicit via LPA 68
Figure 6.1: learning process analysis revealing self-regulation of learning 77
Figure 7.1: Soft skills which can be mapped and analysed
by learning process analysis 80
Figure 7.2: Learning process analysis revealing reasoning 82
Figure 7.3: Learning process analysis revealing collaboration 83
Figure 7.4: Further insight into collaboration using learning
process analysis 84
Figure 7.5: Learning process analysis providing insight
into collaboration 85
Figure 7.6: Learning process analysis revealing
why learners collaborate 86
Figure 7.7: A learner actively managing group dynamics
(revealed via learning process analysis) 86
Figure 7.8: Learning process analysis identifying learners actively
managing the group 87
Figure 7.9: Learning process analysis revealing collaboration
to facilitate learning for the individual and the group 89
Figure 7.10: Learning process analysis revealing listening as part
of learning 90
Figure 7.11: Part of a learning process map illustrating an avenue
to assessment 92
Figure 7.12: Learning process map showing a student's decision-making
and reasons for creating effects in their artwork work 92
Figure 7.13: Learning process map showing nothing available to observe
and all decision-making and reasoning via learning process analysis 94
Figure 7.14 96
Figure 7.15 (2A1) 97
Figures 7.16, 7.17 and 7.18 98
Figure 7.19 99
Figure 7.20 100
Figure 7.21: Social constructivism in action 100

Figure 8.1: Learning process map of a learner in junior science 109
Figure 8.2: Learning process map from a student in a PBL tutorial 110
Figure 8.3: Learning process map with categories 112
Figure 8.4: Shane's learning process map 118
Figure 8.5: Methods of constructing learning process maps 121
Figure 8.6: Learning process map interview sequence 124
Figure 8.7: Learning process map from the above interview transcript 124
Figure 8.8: Part of a proforma from PBL student 125
Figure 8.9: The resultant learning process map derived from the proforma and interview data 126
Figure 8.10: Illustrating some categories of decision-making 131
Figure 8.11: Learning process maps for learner E group session 1 133
Figure 8.12: Learning process maps for learner E group session 2 133
Figure 8.13: Learning process map for exercise 1 145
Figure 8.14: Learning process map for exercise 2 146
Figure 9.1: Learning process map for a manager designing a new human resources program 151
Figure 9.2: Bias versus noise 152
Figure 10.1: Areas where artificial intelligence could play a role in learning process analysis 160

CHAPTER ONE

Introduction

Foreword

In my final year as a trainee teacher at the University of New England (Armidale, Australia). I completed an education elective on Item Response Theory[1] taught by John Hattie and a wonderfully engaging colleague of John's who came from California (I think his name was Bob). The teaching in this unit reflected the message John shares with us today[2]. The classes, still crystal clear in my memory, were vital and engaging. There was a real shared sense among us students (about twelve of us if I recall accurately) that John and Bob wanted to know what we knew and how they could help us know and do more. It was also very clear what their learning intentions[3] for us were, though they were not called by that name back then. John and Bob were beginning to make learning visible—teaching us 'how to know'.

Not too long after that experience, I began working as a teacher brimming with professional enthusiasm, including using the skills and knowledge I had gained from John and Bob's elective. From that point on I have tried to help learners to learn, and to engage with the business of learning. I have endeavoured to keep learning

---

[1] See https://www.sciencedirect.com/topics/social-sciences/item-response-theory
[2] In his book, 'Visible Learning for Teachers: Maximizing impact on learning' (2012), Routledge. New York. John Hattie urges educators to keep learning at the centre of what they do, in particular, helping learners to 'know how to know'.
[3] A term that John uses in his book, above in footnote 2.

at the forefront of what I do. This book is the result of those efforts and my desire to also learn 'how to know', including the research conducted for my doctoral studies.

When I developed learning process analysis[4] as a method for my PhD program over twenty-five years ago, I held the view that the skills learners used were both generic and transferable. I now know that they are not. What I did learn is that learners do use these skills. These skills go by the names: observing, hypothesising, classifying, investigating, collaborating, reflecting and integrating prior knowledge, as some examples. There are other names for these skills, including: investigative skills, learning processes and procedural knowledge. These terms all have different descriptions but they are, in essence, describing much the same thing—what learners are doing when they are trying to learn. Let me show you what I mean with an example.

An example of 'what learners do':

> Take a student in a classroom starting out on an art project. They will draw on prior knowledge; they might observe something out the window. They might recall knowledge of something interesting to them. If working with another student, they might discuss some ideas with each other and decide on a course of action and so on.
>
> Picture a student anywhere doing anything, and you can imagine them using a whole range of skills similar to these but they will differ depending on the context or the subject area.

Learning process analysis gives us access to how learners go about using these skills and because it can do that, it can provide a detailed and accurate evidence base for helping learners to get better at learning.

---

[4] Australian Patent No. 2002313850, 'Learning Process Analysis' (expired December 2022).

INTRODUCTION

A critical feature of learning, and fundamental to the ideas and approaches described in this book, is that learners make conscious and deliberate decisions about how they use these skills. Learning process analysis provides us with access to the decision-making of learners and reveals why they make the decisions they do. That is, it uncovers how learners go about learning.

The central idea of this book is that, by understanding the precise nature of learners' decision-making we are very well placed to provide learners with precise and detailed feedback that will help them get better at learning. This feedback can be used to produce qualitative and quantitative change in learning outcomes. Learning process analysis is a support structure for continual improvement in learning, resulting in greater effectiveness and efficiency for learners. In all instances the goal of this support, one which this book shares, is for learners to:

1. get better at learning (how to know);
2. be consistently better at learning; and
3. achieve better outcomes, more often and more consistently.

I hope this book will inspire you to use the method described within to help make your students' learning more accessible, so that you are better placed to help them learn and that they are better placed 'to know, how to go about knowing and how to do that more efficiently and effectively'[5].

Why is this book important?

Learning can happen at just about any time throughout our lives. If we can get better at learning, and if it can be done effectively and efficiently, then I think this is something we should aim for. This book is important because it describes and explains how to use a proven method that reveals how individuals make decisions when they are learning, playing sport or engaging in work or business.

---

[5] From Hattie, J. 'Visible Learning for Teachers: Maximizing impact on learning' (2012), Routledge. New York.

This book, and the messages contained within, came from my PhD research into learning during which I used a different approach to explore learning. I remember very early on in my research program saying to my supervisor, 'I think learners make decisions as they try to learn'. My supervisor, Mike, wasn't so sure but encouraged me to explore the idea—so off I went. I used the term 'learning process analysis (LPA)'[6] in my PhD research thesis. In essence, what LPA did was map the decision-making processes of learners as they navigated a task. That is, mapping the process of learning. The nature of LPA is to:

- extract the decision-making of learners and the reasons why they make their decisions from beginning to end for each set of decision-making; then
- represent this decision-making, plus reasons, in a way that is accessible to as many people as possible. I chose to develop a map-type structure.

As an example, take a student in a typical learning setting, perhaps a tutorial or a group work session. In either setting any member of the group, on any occasion, might make a whole host of decisions. For instance, they might decide to:

1. ask a question of their colleagues;
2. answer a question asked by a colleague;
3. volunteer to act as a scribe, whether digitally or in-room;
4. look something up because they heard a term which they don't fully understand;
5. stay silent (owing to not understanding some of the content);
6. stay silent (to let others speak); or
7. speak with the facilitator or tutor (to ask a question or to try and manage the group dynamics).

---

[6] This process was what I used in my doctoral research at The University of Sydney (2001). The title of the doctoral thesis was, 'Conceptual Development, Investigative Skills and Decisions about Processes'.

Decisions such as these, that learners make, do not just happen. I know that now. I wasn't at all sure when I first started exploring this area in my PhD research. These things happen in learning settings because learners make conscious decisions to do these things and they do so for very specific reasons. By gaining access to this decision-making and these reasons we can gain a deeper level of understanding of how learners learn (and that they do so in many different ways). With this deeper level of access to learners' thinking we can extract detailed, individualised data about what learners decide to do when they are trying to learn and why they do so.

Let's take one of those decisions I described above.

1. 'Ask a question of their colleagues': a student might ask a question about something a colleague has shared with the group. That same student might ask out loud to the group in search of knowledge. They might ask a very practical question as to whether two research topics could be combined. As I said, these decisions do not just happen. Each question has reasoning behind it. The final question about combining topics might be because the student feels that doing research outside of the group is a valuable learning opportunity. And knowing that precise reason provides us with insight into that learner and how they approached their learning in this context.

Having access to an individual's decision-making and thinking processes can be a significant advantage when providing feedback to a learner about how they can improve what they are doing. That is, to help them get better at learning. In education, learning process analysis provides access to the decision-making of learners. With this sort of access, educators can gain insight into how learners approach their learning and the precise sources of their errors, or indeed, successes.

Let's take that learner from the above example. Say the student's reason was a 'lack of knowledge'. That tells us several things about this learner. It gives us insight into what they know or don't know. It also tells us they are prepared to share a lack of knowledge with their colleagues—which in turn suggests they are open to learning. That is useful information to have about any learner.

Learning process analysis offers a clear way to continued and sustained improvement, potentially more innovative approaches to learning, efficiency in decision-making and consistently better learning results for a student. With ongoing developments in artificial intelligence, learning process analysis offers greater and more targeted opportunities for individualising learning, and I will explore those possibilities later in this book.

In learning, say, small-group learning, you might want all students to contribute to the discussion. For the more silent student one assumption might be that they are not contributing. Using LPA to gain access to a student's decision-making and reasoning, we can make a more precise and accurate assessment of even the silent student in any learning setting. Take the same student above who was asking questions. The following learning process map (Figure 1.1) shows why this learner was being silent:

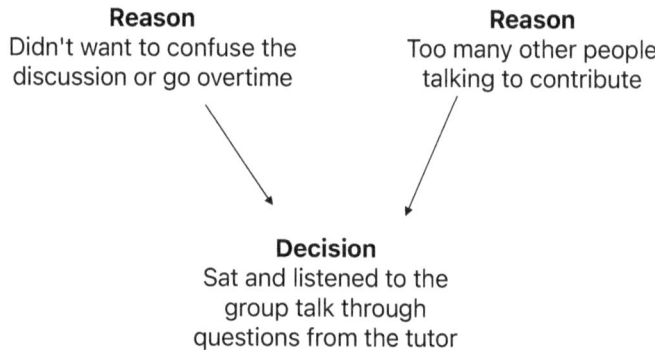

Figure 1.1: An example of a decision with reasoning of the student

The same approach can apply to any group setting, such as a work meeting or a boardroom discussion. This capacity of learning process analysis, to provide access to what individuals are doing and why, has real world potential beyond the classroom. An example of that real world potential is in the development of

INTRODUCTION

soft skills[7]. Business organisations, universities and schools all see the development of what are called soft skills as an important feature of the education system. Workplaces want graduates to have those skills and be able to use them when they enter the workforce. Universities in turn, describe a number of soft skills as expected graduate outcomes. These soft skills include problem solving, critical thinking, communication skills and collaboration as some examples.

Collaboration enables learners to work jointly towards an outcome. Collaboration consists of many behaviours including the identification of a learning issue, silence, asking questions of colleagues or the tutor, explaining, questioning, checking for understanding and recognition of knowledge gaps and acting on that recognition. Poor collaboration is a barrier to successful learning, and for that matter productive workplaces, whilst effective collaboration is seen as necessary for productive learning and working. Learning process analysis can detect who is collaborating, how they are doing so and why in any group situation, whether learning or work. I will discuss this feature of learning process analysis in more detail later in the book. For the moment, let me say this: being able to determine who is collaborating and how and why (asking a question is obvious but knowing why that question is asked is less so) opens up the potential for workplaces to accurately measure collaboration in new hires and also in learning environments. This level of access to decision-making facilitates the development of accurate, measurable and reliable means of detecting soft skills for students and in workplaces.

In summary, what learning process analysis offers, is a different, precise and accurate insight into how people go about making the decisions they do. The overall result is an effective

---

[7] In 2017 Deloitte Australia published a report, 'Soft skills for business success', which made the case for the importance of soft skills in the workplace. Other publications, such as Harvard Business Review, make much the same case about soft skills.

and efficient method which can facilitate the provision of highly accurate feedback to learners about how they learn and how they can become better at learning, and in turn, become more efficient and effective with potentially better outcomes such as: results, better grades, more knowledge, more effectively learned and soft skills acquired and being used more effectively.

Using learning process maps to explore how learners learn

This book describes and makes a case for the adoption of a method called learning process analysis (LPA). Learning process analysis is a method that extracts a person's decision-making and their reasoning behind that decision-making, and represents this information sequentially, step by step, in the form of a learning process map. The resultant learning process map reveals the precise details of an individual's decision-making, making what is generally tacit and unknown, explicit and available for review and analysis.

I used the following diagram earlier which shows what those maps look like and repeat it here:

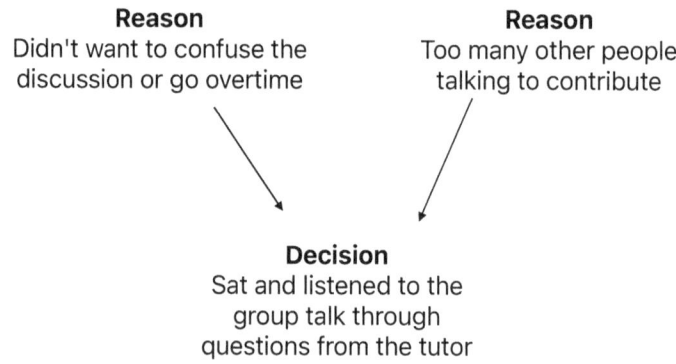

Figure 1.2: An example of a learning process map (decision + reason/s)

One of my key objectives for this book is to describe and explain the overarching principles that underlie LPA. I will also explore insights gained from research which provide additional support for learning process analysis. These principles and insights are important—they are the basis of LPA.

The book is written with three key audiences in mind: people who are learning; people who want to help others to learn; and people who either consult to people who work in learning or conduct research in any area related to learning. That said, I think LPA has applicability beyond these areas and I will discuss those areas throughout the book. Worked examples and descriptions are used to illustrate one of the key messages of this book: that adopting learning process analysis as a feedback tool can produce better outcomes.

I will show you what learning process maps are, how they can be used to your advantage and how to use LPA from beginning to end, including how to analyse and make sense of learning process maps to obtain the greatest advantage from them.

By doing all of these things, I hope you will have gained a real insight and practical knowledge that will provide you with a pathway to continued and sustained improvement and greater efficiency and effectiveness in learning with improved outcomes for your students.

Decision-making—a different perspective

I'd like to sound a note of warning before you venture too far into this book. You are going to meet the term decision-making quite a lot. For you to get the most out of this book you need to think about decision-making in a slightly different way to how it is usually described.

So how is decision-making usually described? Just about every reference you access about decision-making— whether it be slow and fast decision-making (Kahneman)[8], mindful decision-making (lots of people), data-driven decision-making, life decisions and many other takes on decision-making—will describe decision-making a little differently to how it is described in this book. It is not massively different, because we are still talking about decision-making, but it is different. Let me show you how.

---

[8] Daniel Kahneman. 2012 Thinking, Fast and Slow. Penguin Random House. London

With many of these other depictions of decision-making, the focus is on making a specific decision, whether it be you, or you as part of a group of people, such as a boardroom full of directors or colleagues at a work meeting. That focus might be:

- Which car do I purchase (you and maybe others)?
- Do we, as a shared business decision:
   - set up a factory in this location?
   - purchase this land?
   - develop a new product?
- Tossing a coin (heads/tails).

Search online for 'decision-making' and you will come across examples such as these.

Throughout this book I will be describing a different type of decision-making. It is still decision-making in the sense that a person is making a specific decision about something, but in this case, I am exploring the decisions that learners make as they try to learn. This type of decision-making, which you will meet in detail throughout the book, comprises deliberate and conscious decisions made by learners about how they go about a task of any nature. To put it plainly, it is what learners do. Figure 1.1, from earlier in this chapter and repeated below, illustrates this point. This learner decided to sit and listen to her colleagues in the group talk through questions from the tutor.

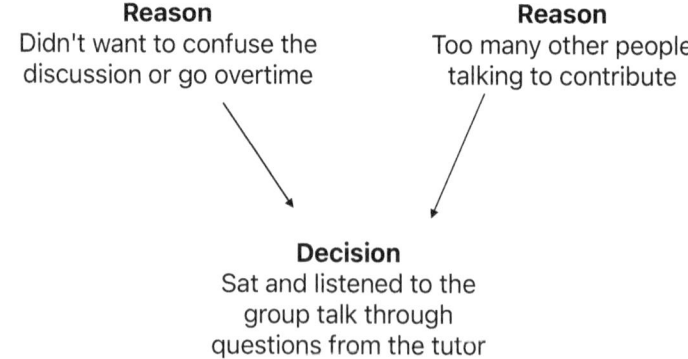

I became interested in this aspect of learning because I think that having a better understanding of how learners approach their learning is one avenue to helping learners to get better at it. Let us see how that works out.

Getting better at learning

For the most part, we all want to get better at what we do, no matter what that might be. The motivation for doing so comes from all areas of our lives. It might be a promotion at work or at least the prospect of one. It might be excelling at school or university (or it might just be passing) and the prospects that success will bring. We tend to get better through learning. Getting better at learning is really getting better at knowing things. It is also about getting better at knowing how to learn.

To get better we try whatever we think will help us to do so. We read books (like this one), read blogs, listen to podcasts, subscribe to feeds, seek feedback, join groups in-person and online and talk to our family and trusted friends. We might occasionally talk to ourselves, maybe to our pets and sometimes to complete strangers. We go to conferences, enrol in learning courses or practise wellness. We train and practice skills—the list is long and seemingly endless. Over our many journeys of learning we invest time, energy and sometimes money, in the name of continual improvement. Trying to get better through learning, and at learning, means something to us, and that is a good thing. It should, because learning is more than just something that happens in your head; it is also about how you feel. For the purposes of this book, I am going to assume that you either want to get better at learning, or you want to help others to get better at learning.

So how does this book help you to get better at learning? What I want to do through this book is to show you how you can get better (and/or help others to get better) at knowing things (i.e. learning), consistently and with confidence by using learning process analysis.

Learning process analysis to generate feedback

It is generally accepted that to get better at learning, or just about anything, you require feedback on your performance. That cycle of improvement consists of trying to learn, measuring performance in some way, receiving feedback, making sense of that feedback with or without the help of others and then responding in some way to that feedback. Feedback is based on the output of learners. That output can be from just about anything including quizzes, assignments, art works and other products or outcomes of learners as well as performance-based assessments. Just about anything really. It depends on what is being learned. There is increasing interest in understanding how learners learn. One particular focus is on trying to better understand in real time how learners approach their learning. That is, trying to understand what learners are doing when they are trying to learn. In the past, much of these attempts to understand learning came from self-report surveys that learners completed. These sorts of surveys ask people what they thought about what they were doing, mostly after the event.

Using microanalysis as a basis for feedback

An alternative to self-report surveys is to assess learners in real time as they engage in learning tasks, including assessment tasks—what researchers of learning call microanalysis. There are various types of microanalyses, such as those targeting the strategies of learners to manage their learning. Learning process analysis, the subject of this book, is a new and different form of microanalysis that focuses on how learners learn. As John Hattie and Gregory Donohue have described it: the focus of education is on helping learners: 'how to know, how to know more efficiently and how to know more effectively.'[9] By focusing on how learners learn in real time, learning process analysis can play a role in helping learners to do these things.

---

[9] JAC Hattie & GM Donohue 2016 Learning strategies: a synthesis and conceptual model. npj Science of Learning. 1. 13. Published online 10 August 2016.

The business of learning

I use the term 'business of learning' throughout this book. I do so because I think this phrase better captures all those who are engaged in learning, plus those who might be somewhat less engaged in learning. Learning process analysis works on the principles that as learners go about the business of learning, they make a whole series of decisions about how they do that and for all these decisions made, learners have very clear and precise reasons why they make those decisions. These underlying principles of learning process analysis are based on research and what we know about learning. I will describe and explain these underlying principles and how they work to support learning process analysis in chapter 4.

Learning as a purposeful activity

Learning is a purposeful activity. People do not learn by accident. Learning generally plays out in the following way: learners make decisions about what they are going to do; why they are doing these things and where relevant, where, when and with whom they are doing something, and from that series of decisions there are outcomes, sometimes pleasing, sometimes less so. If you want to pare learning back to the absolute basics to better understand how learners learn, and therefore, be in a better position to help learners get better at 'how to know', then looking at the decisions learners make is a good place to start. A greater understanding of what these decisions are, what role they play in learning and why learners make the decisions they do is exactly what learning process analysis offers as a means of better understanding learning.

> **Case study of learning
> (and how learning process analysis can help)**
>
> Take Stephen, for example. Stephen is a student in a problem-based learning (PBL) tutorial. The tutor notices that Stephen seems to say very little. On the surface (i.e. what we observe) what we have is a quiet, maybe reflective student. Yet that is, in effect, guesswork—we don't really know what Stephen's approach to learning is and how that plays out. Using learning process analysis as an auditing tool will reveal that Stephen, at least in this instance, is enabling others to speak because he thinks it is in the best interests of the group and suits the way he prefers to learn. A learning process map (Figure 1.3) reveals the true nature of Stephen's approach to learning.

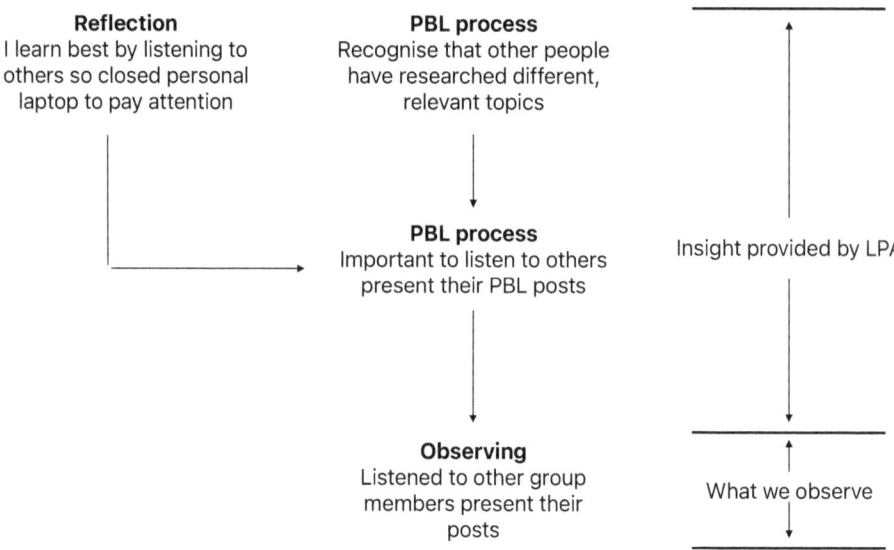

Figure 1.3: Learning process map of Stephen in a problem-based learning (PBL) tutorial

What we learn from Stephen's learning process map is that Stephen is making decisions about how he will get the best learning value out of this tutorial. What we also learn, courtesy of learning process analysis, is that Stephen is self-regulating his learning. That is, he is appraising the situation and making a decision about how he will approach a task during the tutorial in order to facilitate his learning. Stephen's decision-making is not an isolated instance in learning. Many other learners, just about all in fact, make these sorts of decisions throughout their learning journeys. We can also see the utility of learning process analysis as a method. To the observer, Stephen is potentially listening due to having closed his laptop. That is all we can tell by observing visually. What learning process analysis adds to this picture is that there are several decisions made by Stephen, providing insight into how he learns and why he does so. It is this insight that can provide the basis for detailed feedback to both learners and educators.

It's not about decision-making—it's about learning

This book is about learning and helping learners to get better at it by employing the learning process analysis method. Although you will meet the terms decision-making and decisions at regular intervals, this book is not about understanding decision-making. Accessing learners' decision-making is a means to an end. The means is that by extracting learners' decision-making, their reasons for those decisions, categorising this data and mapping it helps us make sense of how learners learn. And that will continue for as long as someone is learning. Let me spell that out for you (see Figure 1.4):

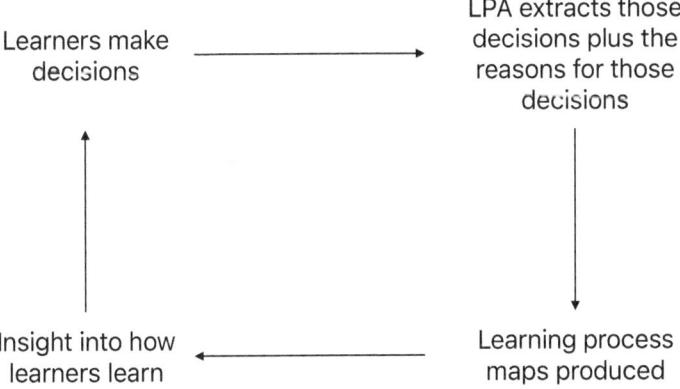

Figure 1.4: LPA and how it works

The end, as it were, is to assist learners to get better at learning, not because they are making better decisions but because they are making different decisions. This point is an important distinction to keep in mind for learning process analysis. The goal is to help learners to make different decisions that result in more effective and efficient learning, and to better understand how to help each learner to improve how they learn. That doesn't mean a learner will never make a mistake again. They will, and courtesy of learning process analysis we and the learner can continue to gain insight into their approach to learning. The term lifelong learning is bandied about with increasing regularity. Yet it is true. We are constantly reviewing how we approach any number of tasks to get better at whatever we are doing and this is very much the case whether we are in the classroom or the workplace. We can all benefit from getting better at learning.

Be careful of being offered opportunities for you or your learners to make better decisions. I'm afraid that place just doesn't exist. The first question you might ask someone offering such an opportunity is, how do you determine that one decision is better than another? And if the answer is 'better outcomes' that is because the learner is making different decisions, has received feedback and has learned something. As I hope you will see: what we have is learners making decisions and it is these decisions that represent how learners approach their learning.

Keep the principle of 'it's not about decision-making, it's about learning' at the forefront of your thinking as you read this book and eventually try out learning process analysis for yourself. By doing so I think you will gain the maximum benefit from this book.

How do we get better at learning?

So, how do we get better and what do we need to get better at and how often do we need to get better? Every day? All the time? Just in some areas and not others? Important questions and best answered by you. For the purposes of this book, I will assume you either want to get better at learning and/or you want to help others to do so. We need to start with what learning even means. Where does it occur? How do learners go about trying to learn? This book has been written to show you that by examining learners' decision-making in detail and in particular about how they approach learning, then we can better understand these aspects of learning. To make the most of this book we need to understand what that decision-making is. We need to know how it works, how we can best detect it, how we can make sense of it and how we can best feed this information about decision-making to learners to help them get better at learning. In a nutshell, learning process analysis may be thought of as a method that accesses the tacit process of a learner's decisions and makes this information explicit and accessible.

The book will guide you step-by-step, showing you how to use the learning process analysis method to extract, map and analyse the decision-making of learners. I will briefly describe some examples below to illustrate how learning process analysis can help you.

Classroom and learning environments consist of individuals with different beliefs, values, skill sets, understanding of concepts and ideas and interests. These differences are often the driving forces behind why decisions are made and influence learners' approaches to learning. Having reliable and accurate insight into why learners make the decisions they do and the role these differences play using LPA, provides educators with the capacity to conduct a forensic analysis of how learners learn.

It is my fervent hope that learning process analysis can go some way to contributing to education, learning and positively impact the outcomes of learning for learners of all ages, in any learning situation.

An example of learning process analysis in action

What follows is an example drawn from a student participating in a small-group tutorial. In this instance the student is contributing to the group discussion. Her decision was to:

1. 'talk about different systems involved in each symptom'.

For this decision the student offered several reasons and described how she contributed to the group. The reasons were:

a. 'important to explore symptoms to get an idea of what is going on'; and
b. 'useful to link all of the parts of the body together and pathways of pathophysiology'.

And she made the decision by speaking:

a. 'aloud to the group'.

Figure 1.5 shows this sequence of reasoning and decision-making (i.e. a learning process map).

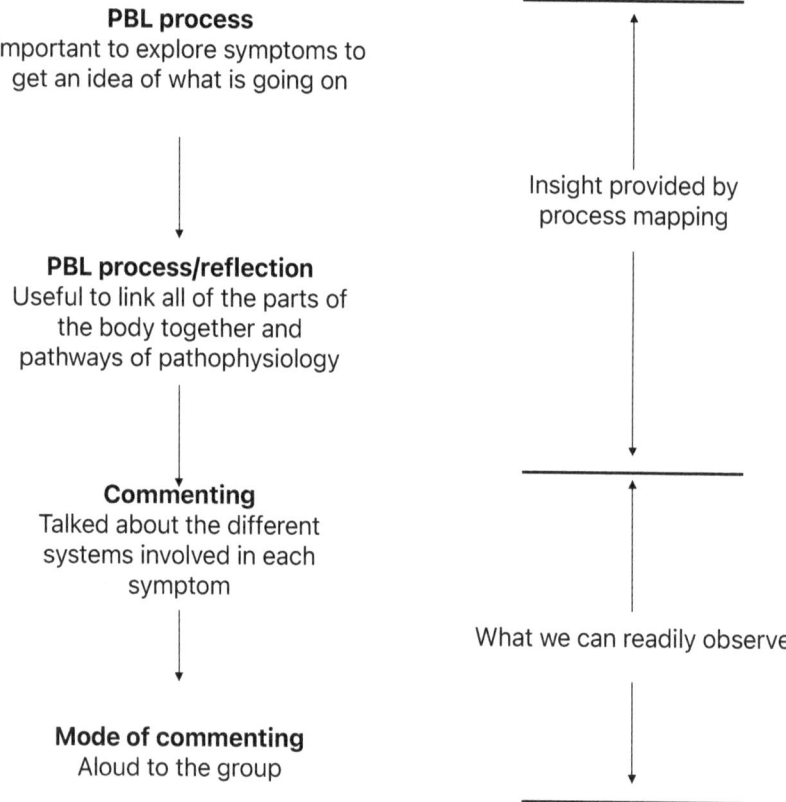

Figure 1.5: Learning process map for a student in a small-group tutorial

INTRODUCTION

The value proposition of learning process analysis

The value proposition of learning process analysis comes from its capacity to provide explicit detail to both the learner and the educator about how a learner approaches a task and why they approached the task the way they did. It does that visually in flowchart form (a learning process map), making it easier to review a learner's approach to a task. When we observe learners learning we see what I would call the surface features of learning: talking, listening, using a laptop and many other observable actions. Learning process analysis reveals what is below that surface layer, revealing details not previously understood or easily attainable (see figures 1.2 and 1.4 above). To use an analogy, what we see on the surface is the equivalent of the duck on the water, whilst underneath, courtesy of learning process analysis, we see the multiple instances of decision-making that maintain the smooth appearance of learning on the surface.

You wouldn't use learning process analysis for every decision, or indeed every task. To do so would most likely be unproductive and ineffective. You might though conduct an audit or review of decision-making in a targeted way as part of an overall strategic goal to long-term improvement of either an individual learner or a group of learners (for instance, learners whose progress is at risk). The choices are entirely yours to make.

As described briefly in the introduction, one area where learning process analysis can play a role is an area commonly called 'soft skills'. Business is increasingly recognising the importance of these skills and the value they offer to an organisation to the extent that training, including that on soft skills, is a multi-billion-dollar enterprise. Organisations that rely on people having soft skills are increasing and, with the ongoing development in artificial intelligence applications and machine learning, these soft skills are becoming more relevant by the day[10]. Education, in all its

---

[10] By way of example see, The Soft Skills of Great Digital Organisations, Harvard Business Review, February 5, 2016

forms—school, university, training organisations, in-house training facilities with large organisations—need to be ready to contribute to the ongoing development and management of people's soft skills.

Organisations, including Forbes, Deloitte and Harvard Business School, have nominated a number of soft skills as important to the future. These soft skills include: problem solving, self-management and regulation, critical thinking, collaboration and teamwork, judgement and complex decision-making, interpersonal communication skills, professional ethical behaviour, an ability to learn ('how to know' in the parlance of John Hattie and Chris Donohue[11]) and innovation. The expectation from business and the workforce is that students, graduating from school, post-school education and even short courses run by human resource departments or professional training organisations, will be equipped with an ever-increasing array of these skills and the capacity to use them as required. Learning organisations need to be both equipped and positioned to play a key role in detecting and improving these soft skills.

Soft skills are considered to be hard to measure. One reason why people have reached this view is a lack of tools or methods that can accurately reveal the detail of an individual's soft skills and how they use these soft skills. Both elements are required if we are to better understand the nature of the day-to-day business of work, soft skills and people. Decision-making is central to the use of these soft skills. Take collaboration and/or teamwork as an example. People, including learners, make conscious decisions to collaborate, or indeed to not collaborate with others, whether that is in a small group or a larger set-up. They will also make conscious decisions about how to go about collaborating. On top of that, learners (and people in the real world) will actively decide when to collaborate and with whom and will have clear reasons why they do or don't collaborate. These conscious and deliberate

---

[11] Hattie, J. A. C., & Donoghue, G. M. (2016). Learning strategies: a synthesis and conceptual model. *npj Science of Learning*, 1, 16013. https://doi.org/10.1038/npjscilearn.2016.13

decisions to collaborate, how to do so, with whom and when, will be made for specific and identifiable reasons. It is this factor, having reasons for making a decision to collaborate or not, that enables learning process analysis to play a key role in identifying how people are collaborating and why they are doing so.

LPA can be used in this way for any of the soft skills desired by business, and ultimately will be beneficial for learners giving them greater scope to work in organisations that demand these soft skills. This capacity to map soft skill use in detail can be further developed by incorporating learning process analysis into professional qualifications so that institutions could develop a soft skill passport for each student, which can verify attainment and development in a list of nominated soft skills. These unique features will be explored in more detail in chapter six.

Another very useful application of learning process analysis, again introduced here and explored in detail in chapter six, is that it can provide both quantitative and qualitative analyses of how people use soft skills. Using learning process analysis in these ways can be done at either the organisational or individual level.

John Hattie, in calling for learning to be more visible in his book *Visible Learning for Teachers* (2016), urges educators to keep learning at the front and centre of what they do. Learning, after all, is the main game at all levels of education. The notion of learning being more visible, easier to 'see' if you like, is a very useful and interesting idea because learning is what education is about. These aspects and applications of learning process analysis will be described and explained in full in chapter six.

The following people should read this book:

- Anyone interested in learning at any level, in any area, for whatever reason.
- Organisations engaged in education from primary to post-graduate.
- Any training organisation that either offers learning, whether as micro-credentials or longer-term credentials,

to other organisations, or to its own people as part of in-house training.
- Private groups that also educate people including such organisations as the Institute of Directors (UK) and the Australian Institute of Company Directors (AICD) as two examples. There are many more.
- Developers of information technology systems including artificial intelligence and machine learning, where understanding learning and being able to map decision-making, especially general artificial intelligence systems, can inform future developments.
- Professions (mostly distributed throughout the first three areas above) including law, engineering, medicine and allied health, defence, professional sport, education and their associated organisations.
- People who consult to organisations, conduct research in education, learning or any of the above professional areas.

I hope you all benefit—that is my goal.

Throughout this book a range of examples from education, and occasionally business, will be used to illustrate how learning process analysis can make a difference to you and/or your organisation by revealing how people approach learning. In detail, the following sections will:

- describe the learning process analysis method; and
- describe and explain the overarching principles and illustrate how these principles, when combined with several general insights gained from research, underpin and support learning process analysis.

Subsequent sections will:

- illustrate in detail the insights that learning process analysis reveals; and
- walk you through, step-by-step the entire method including:

- capturing the initial data;
- interviewing individuals to confirm these data and capture additional data (if any);
- constructing learning process maps;
- categorising the decisions, observations and reasons that form the individual elements of a learning process map;
- analysing learning process maps; and
- how best to use the outcomes of that analysis.

The final section explores the opportunities and possibilities learning process analysis might offer beyond that explored in previous chapters. Some of these possibilities include integration of learning process analysis into software; utilising learning process analysis in artificial intelligence and machine learning; and employing learning process analysis as a research method and analytical tool for any of the areas explored in this book and beyond.

I hope you will find this book and its contents useful, for both you and/or your learners, and urge you to consider and pursue other uses and analyses not presented in this book, knowing the foundations of learning process analysis are there to support you in your endeavours. My vision is for this book to be taken up in any area and for learning process analysis to be adopted as a market-leading approach driving individual and/or organisational improvement, resulting in an improved bottom line, however that bottom line is measured.

CHAPTER TWO

Learning process maps and how they work

What is a learning process map?

Learning process maps are graphical tools for organising and representing the decision-making of learners as they engage in a task. The initial function of a learning process map is that it visibly represents learners' decisions sequentially. Each learning process map represents a learner's decision, or decisions, and any reasons they had for those decisions. Learning process maps provide a means of illustrating how learners' decisions relate to each other. They are also designed to compare the decisions learners make about processes, from one learning event to the next[12].

The components of a learning process map

A learning process map has two key components. One component is a decision made by a learner. The second component is the reason for each decision. These two components are set out similarly to how nodes (concepts) are in a concept map[13] with a connecting arrow showing the progression of a learner's decision-making. Learners' decisions and the reasons for them are presented sequentially from the initial decision or reason for a decision to

---

[12] Corrigan G. 2001. Conceptual development, investigative skills and decisions about processes. [PhD dissertation]. Sydney. The University of Sydney.

[13] See Novak, J.D. and Gowin, D.B. (1984) Learning How to Learn. Cambridge: Cambridge University Press. Novak and Gowin developed concept mapping and describe what it is and how it works in this book.

the final decision (see Figure 2.1) and indicated by the direction of the arrows.

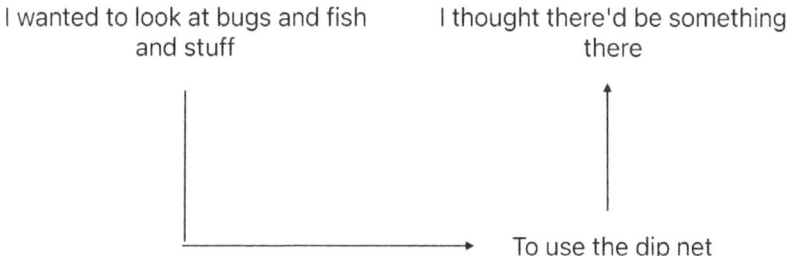

Figure 2.1: Learning process map showing sequential direction

How do you 'read' a learning process map?

When you are starting out with learning process analysis, I recommend reading a learning process map in the direction of the arrows. The example above (figure 2.1) is taken from my PhD research, where junior science students were asked to explore the relationships between the environment and living things. This activity was undertaken at a field studies centre, with both the task and the setting designed to maximise the potential for students to make decisions about how they went about their learning. The field studies centre had a wide range of equipment for the students to use, including dip nets.

In terms of reading a learning process map and using the example above in Figure 2.1, you would read it in the following way:

1. Because I wanted to look at bugs and fish and stuff.
2. AND
3. Because I thought there would be something there.
4. I decided to use the dip net.

If you convert this series of steps into a normal sentence structure, it would read as follows: Student A decided to use the dip net because they wanted to look at bugs and stuff and because they thought something would be there.

Another example of reading a learning process map is below, along with the accompanying learning process map (Figure 2.2). This learning process map is taken from a graduate entry medical student during a PBL tutorial. In this instance the student is describing concepts that form part of the PBL learning environment. Typically, in PBL tutorials students are trying to make sense of how a patient presents (the presentation) to a doctor. The patient might present with particular symptoms or signs, like a raised body temperature. One of the goals of PBL is for students to be able to describe and explain what is happening in the body (the mechanism). In what is a very busy learning environment, another expectation is that once an accurate diagnosis of the presentation is made students will collaboratively establish how best to look after that patient (how to manage the patient, hence management). Colloquially we might talk about treating a problem. Medical students are taught to think more broadly than that, including social and behavioural support for patients as part of helping the patient.

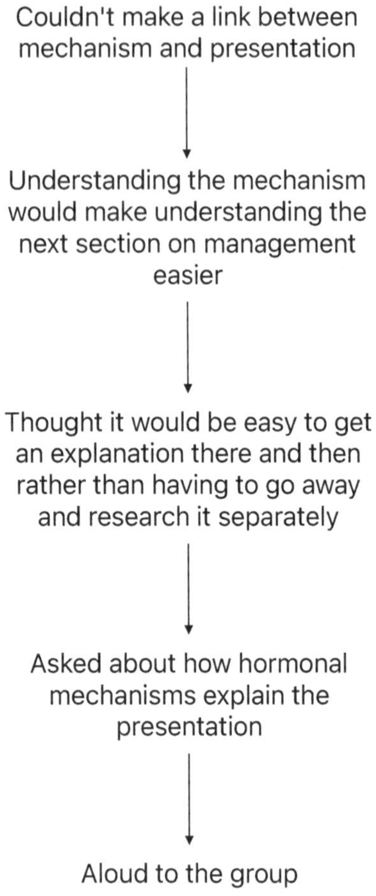

Couldn't make a link between mechanism and presentation

↓

Understanding the mechanism would make understanding the next section on management easier

↓

Thought it would be easy to get an explanation there and then rather than having to go away and research it separately

↓

Asked about how hormonal mechanisms explain the presentation

↓

Aloud to the group

Figure 2.2: Learning process map showing sequential direction

The learning process map in figure 2.2 above is read as follows:

1. because I couldn't make a link between (the) mechanism and (the) presentation; and

2. because understanding the mechanism would make understanding the next section on management easier; and
3. because I thought it would be easier to get an explanation then and there rather than have to go away and research it separately:
4. I asked about how hormonal mechanisms explain the presentation; and
5. I did so aloud to the group.

There are differences between this map and the previous one. The more obvious feature is a more complex set of reasoning (three reasons) for what seems a fairly straightforward decision: to ask a question in a small group tutorial. I will explore these aspects of learning process analysis and these types of differences in more detail in chapter six.

Making sense of a learning process map

To make sense of a learning process map you will need to understand: the process of categorising decisions and reasons for decisions; what learners make decisions about; how you collect the data to produce a concept map; and how you put all of this together in constructing a learning process map. What follows is an introduction to these aspects of learning process analysis.

Categorising learners' decisions and their reasons for their decisions

Most collections of just about anything end up being classified into categories. It would appear to be something that we humans do. As it is with learners' decision-making and the reasons they have for their decisions. One of the features of any classification scheme is an attempt to place some order into what we have in front of us. Most classification schemes have an underlying basis and a particular nomenclature. My suggested classification scheme for learning process analysis and the contents of learning process maps is no different to this general approach to classifying things. I will describe it below.

The categorisation of key elements of a learning process map, decisions and reasons for decisions, is based on the nature of the decision-making and what we know about learning. These categories are initially based on the type of decision (1st division), then the specific decision itself (2nd division) and the 3rd division is the reason, or reasons, for a specific decision. There are classifications (types) of decisions in each division.

The 1st division has four classifications:

- a decision **to do something**;
- a decision about **how to do something**;
- a decision about **when to do something**; and
- a decision about **where to do something**.

Not all of these types of decisions will be used every time a learner engages in learning but they can be. The first two types, to do something and how to do something, are the most common decision types.

The 2nd division is made up of the specific decisions made *within* each of the above four classifications. For example, a decision to do something (division 1) might be 'to look up the meaning of ...'. Another example would be a decision to do something (division 1) and how to do something; the how decision is, 'to look it up on Google' (division 2).

Other examples include, deciding to:

- hypothesise,
- ask a question,
- observe,
- source information,
- comment,
- stay silent and listen,
- think about the dynamics of the learning environment,
- extract from experience,
- reflect,

- prioritise key information,
- deduce,
- infer,
- prioritise patient-centred care,
- recall stored knowledge,
- self-direct learning,
- self-regulate learning,
- assign differential diagnoses,
- make a management decision and
- think about learning.

The 3rd division, the reason or reasons why a decision is made, will vary considerably, almost to the point they might be completely idiosyncratic to a particular learner. These reasons are an important component when constructing learning process maps and also in understanding and interpreting them.

Some examples of this taxonomy, presented as learning process maps, are provided below (Figures 2.3a, Figure 2.3b and Figure 2.3c).

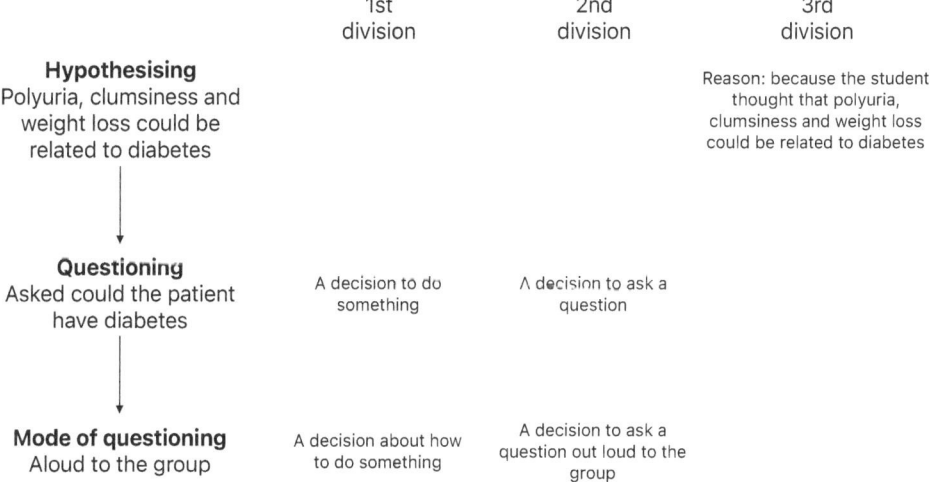

Figure 2.3a: Taxonomic divisions in LPA

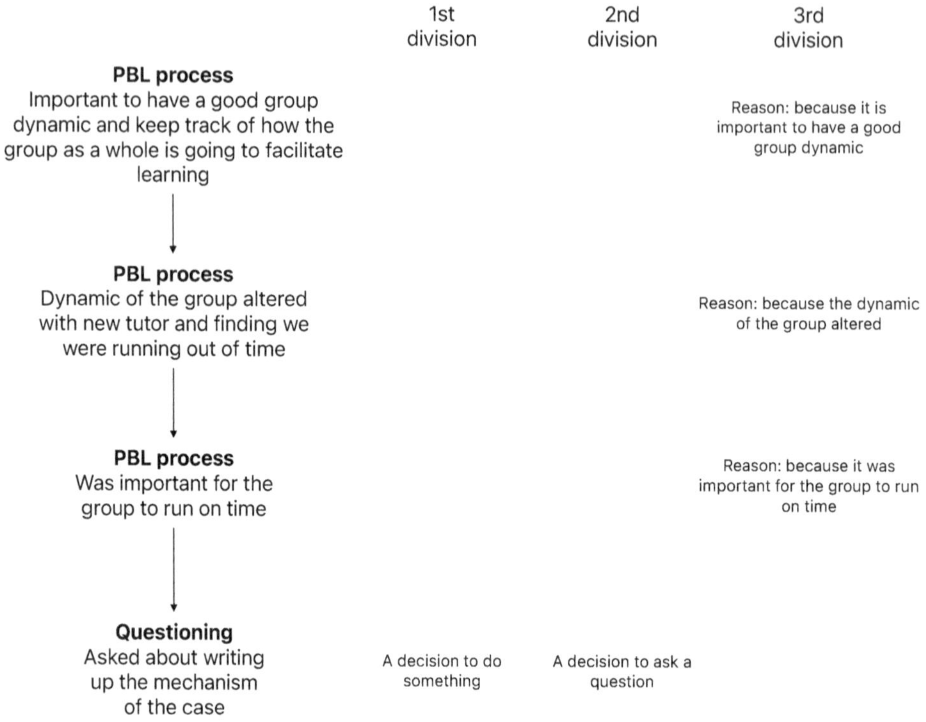

	1st division	2nd division	3rd division
PBL process Important to have a good group dynamic and keep track of how the group as a whole is going to facilitate learning			Reason: because it is important to have a good group dynamic
↓			
PBL process Dynamic of the group altered with new tutor and finding we were running out of time			Reason: because the dynamic of the group altered
↓			
PBL process Was important for the group to run on time			Reason: because it was important for the group to run on time
↓			
Questioning Asked about writing up the mechanism of the case	A decision to do something	A decision to ask a question	

Figure 2.3b: Taxonomic divisions in LPA

	1st division	2nd division	3rd division
PBL process Important to learn clinical reasoning for real patients to address their concerns and make valid diagnostic decisions			Reason: because it is important to learn clinical reasoning for real patients to address their concerns
↓			
PBL process Important to keep key features of the case in mind and cover off all of the presenting symptoms			Reason: because it is important to keep key features of the case in mind
↓			
Observing Listened to colleague re-cap the session	A decision to do something	A decision to observe (listen)	

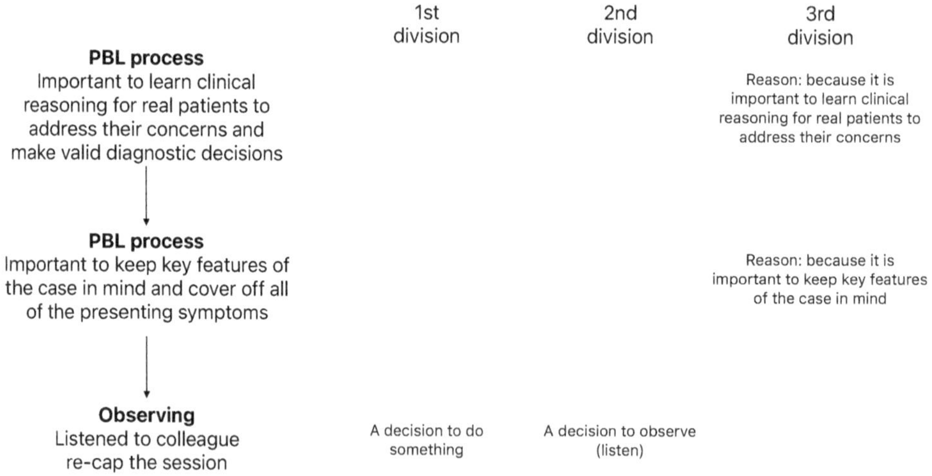

Figure 2.3c: Taxonomic divisions in LPA

Constructing a learning process map

To construct a learning process map the first thing you need to do is to extract learners' decisions and their reasons for these decisions. The method has four steps:

1. extract learners' decisions;
2. drill down into their reasons including uncovering decisions not brought to light in the first step;
3. construct the map sequentially so that it reads from either top to bottom or left to right (or any other alternatives, as long as the direction of decision-making is clear using arrows); and finally,
4. categorise and classify the decisions and reasons.

The final product, a learning process map, resembles a flow chart (refer to any of the learning process maps immediately above to see the similarity).

Step 1: to extract learners' decisions

The simplest way of extracting decisions is to use a proforma. Using the proforma, learners write down the decisions they make as they undertake a learning task.

Step 2: to extract learners' decisions

The second step, interviewing the learner, based on their proforma, is best done and is most effective if completed within 24 hours of the student completing the proforma. The full set of steps are outlined in figure 2.4 below.

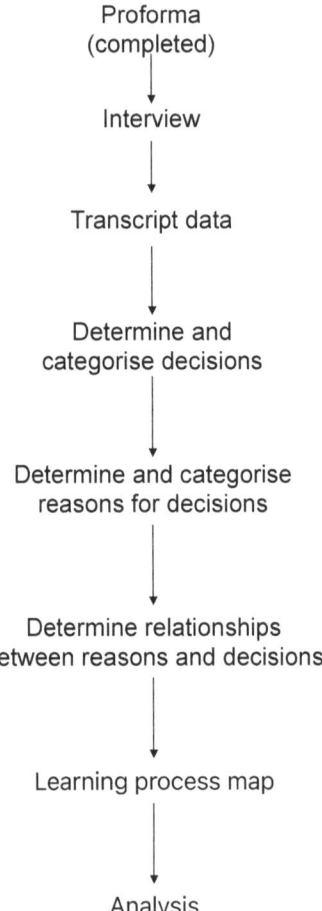

Figure 2.4: The steps required to construct a learning process map

A couple of detailed examples of this process including the completed proforma, interview data and final learning process maps (examples) are provided below – one from a Year 5 art task and the other from a problem-based learning tutorial in medicine.

Year 5 Art task

Proforma (step 1): The proforma took the shape of an 'Art Project Diary' and the instructions were, 'to write down your decisions as you work on your art project.'

> **My Art Project Diary**
>
> Things I did
>
> My partner and I decided to do our project as photography but then changed our decision to do a painting
>
> We then chose to do our project on a tree with a sunset behind it. Originally we were going to paint the sunset and draw the tree but my partner thought of an idea where we blow the paint with a straw to create a tree figure, and I thought it was a good idea
>
> ...so we decided to do it
>
> I made a basic draft of the painting and then went on to make a more distinct draft of the painting with labelling
>
> We got a piece of paper to see the effect of the water colour on the page
>
> We painted the tree instead of using a straw to see the effect
>
> We decided to not use the straw and paint the tree instead

Figure 2.5: A student's returned proforma (reconstructed)

The interview (step 2): Using the proforma as a basis for drilling down deeper into the decision-making of the learner including their reasons for making decisions.

Interviewer: This one here says, 'my partner and I decided to do our project as photography but then changed our decision to do a painting'. Why did you do that, do you think?

Student: Because we thought it might be a little bit easier and it might look a bit nicer.

Interviewer: Then you went on here it says, 'we then chose to do our project on a tree with a sunset behind it.'

Student:	Originally, we were going to paint the sunset and draw the tree but my partner thought of an idea where we blow the paint with a straw to create the tree figure and I thought it was a good idea.
Interviewer:	What decision are you making here?
Student:	We decided to do the painting a little bit different to make it more effective.
Interviewer:	Okay, so you wanted it to be different and what was the choice then to make it more different? What did you choose to do then?
Student:	We chose to like use a straw to like blow a paint to make like a tree effect.
Interviewer:	Okay so you went and got the straw. What did you do after you went and got the straw?
Student:	Well before that we made a basic draft of the painting in our art books. Yes, and then we made another draft with like more labelling and what we need.
Interviewer:	Okay so you did that draft of it in your art book then once you got that done what did you do?
Student:	We got a piece of paper.
Interviewer:	What were your thoughts then once you got your paper what did you think you'd do then?
Student:	We thought we might like try and paint it to see what the effect would be like.
Interviewer:	Okay and paint what?
Student:	The sunset and yeah.
Interviewer:	Okay, so I did see you painting the background. What did you do after that? What decision?
Student:	We painted the tree instead of using the straw just to see what it would look like.

Interviewer:	So, once you painted the tree instead of using the straw to blow the paint on, because you wanted to see the effect of having a real tree there, what did you think and what did you decide to do then?		
Student:	We kind of changed our decision to, yeah, to change the decision.		
Interviewer:	So you've done that, so was that good enough or did you go and do anything else then or what?		
Student:	No, we didn't go into anything else, yeah.		

Step 3: constructing the learning process map

Please see the table below.

Details of step	Possible to standardise and/or automate?	How?	Comment, with a view to development
Step 1 Obtain initial data (decisions made and reasons why these decisions were made).	Yes	Using template, proforma or video.	Template can be paper/electronically based. Step 1 lends itself to an online interface and is the first step required. Decisions and reasons why are required for the construction of learning process maps.
Step 2 Drill down into all decisions and reasons exploring underlying reasons that were made and any decisions not brought out in step 1.	Yes	Interactive, stimulated recall interview.	Step 2 requires identification of decisions and reasons that need to be followed up. Standard follow-up questions are 'why did you make that decision?'; 'was there another reason?'; 'why ...?'. This step can be completed either verbally or in written form and either in person or remotely. Responses are added to data that forms the basis of learning process maps.

| Step 3
Construct decision pathways with data obtained from steps 1 and 2 | Yes
Currently not automated | Using a drawing tool (need to be able to convert text to flowchart, in correct order with correct relationship between decisions and reasons). | Anything that has a drawing function (including pencil and paper). Currently step 3 is a learned skill and can be acquired. |
| --- | --- | --- | --- |
| Step 4
Analysis and feedback | Yes
Currently not | By referring to the learning process maps and assessing the complexity of the decisions and reasons and linkages. | This step requires volume of data and assessment through analysis of the learning process map. Can be done manually at present. Currently a learned skill and can be acquired. |

Table 2.1: The steps required to construct a learning process map

Constructing a learning process map can be done with or without the use of technology. Drawing your maps by hand offers the same opportunities to make sense of a learner's decision-making, as does a computer/device generated version.

From the above data (completed proforma and interview data) the following learning process map is produced.

LEARNING PROCESS MAPS AND HOW THEY WORK

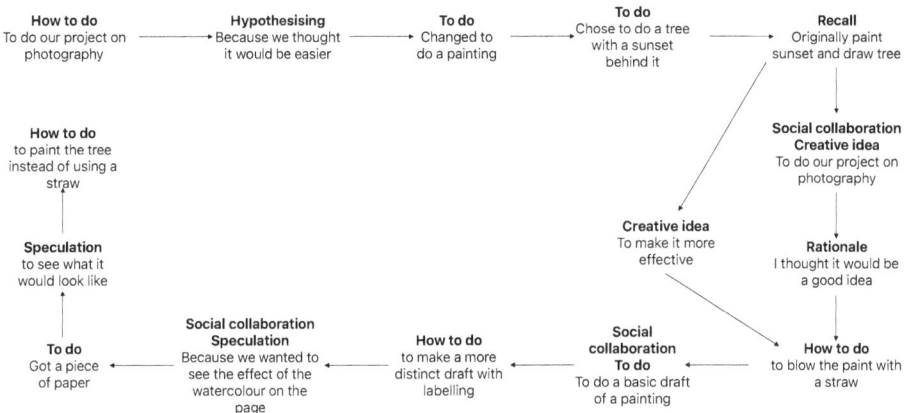

Figure 2.6: A learning process map developed from the above proforma and interview

Step 4: categorising the decisions and reasons in a learning process map

All parts of a learning process map can be categorised. The purpose of categorising decisions and the associated reasons is not to place some arbitrary category on what learners are doing. Rather, it is to better understand what learners are doing, using established concepts in learning as the basis for these categories and to facilitate constructive feedback designed to help learners get better at learning.

CHAPTER THREE

Learning process analysis for learning

What learning process analysis can do

If you had the privilege of observing learners in a learning setting, what you see would vary considerably. They might be quietly sitting around a table, maybe speaking with each other, maybe not. They might be actively engaged in vigorous discussion with each other and/or their teacher. They might be sitting at home listening or watching something relevant to their current learning. They might even be taking part in an online tutorial while sitting in the back seat of their parent's car heading to the coast. Or they might be silently contemplating what other materials they might incorporate into their sculpture. In all these instances and just about any other setting you can imagine, these are learners engaged in learning. This engagement is part of what I have called the 'business of learning'.

Learning settings have always been varied and will continue to be. This variation makes it all the more important to have a reliable means of understanding how each learner learns. We need to understand how learners truly learn if we are to provide them with the detailed and precise feedback that will help them to get better at learning.

John Hattie is an experienced and award-winning researcher and author in education who has published broadly and successfully, including his series of Visible Learning publications. In calling for learning to be more visible, in his book *Visible*

Learning for Teachers (2016), John Hattie urges educators to keep learning at the front and centre of what they do. Increased visibility of learning, in any form, offers the potential for greater insight into what learners do when they go about the business of learning.

Increasing the visibility of learning

Greater visibility can play a significant role in helping to keep learning at the centre of what educators do. John Hattie and Gregory Donohue's description, 'how to know, how to know more efficiently and how to know more effectively' in their 2016 publication nicely captures the 'business of learning'. Learning process analysis is designed to assist in making learning visible—and the more ways we can provide visibility the more opportunities we have to help learners get better at the business of learning.

How can we best achieve this increased visibility? What would that greater visibility look like? What would we see? What is being made visible that was previously invisible? What sort of insight can LPA deliver? How will this insight help learners learn and assist you in managing their learning? The place to start is the reason why teachers turn up to work every day—students.

For any group of learners, at any stage of learning, there will be significant variability in their motivation, their knowledge and also their capacity to employ a range of skills, such as problem-solving, synthesising, critically analysing and/or their capacity to describe what they have learned. It is this variability that is both the challenge and the beauty of teaching—motivating teachers, noting learners' differences, detecting similarities across the group or groups and working with learners to help them learn. As part of the challenge of teaching you are trying to cater for all learners, or at least as many as you can realistically cater for, in a busy classroom, from day to day and for weeks on end. For those less familiar with teaching, including those of you who might be thinking of being a teacher, it also contributes to the immeasurable joy of teaching, particularly when you can meet that challenge, even part of the way, and see the results. It is my earnest hope that this book will help you meet those challenges with greater assurance and you will feel that joy more often, without adding to the complexity or busyness of your teaching day.

Variability in learning outcomes

Within any learning environment you are likely to have a set of stated learning intentions, sometimes called learning outcomes or objectives. For the purposes of this book, what they are called does not particularly matter. What does matter is that typically, no matter the age of the learner or the type of learning environment, you will not find common achievement of these learning intentions. This spread of achievement is evident in the distribution of results in any subject, at any stage of learning. This variation in learning outcomes comes from a range of sources including, but not limited to, variability in the knowledge and skill levels of the learners. No big surprise there—variability in knowledge and skill levels, amongst other things, produces variability in measured results. So where does that leave us in our desire to help learners get better at learning?

Detecting variability in knowledge is a fairly straightforward task and there are multiple ways of measuring knowledge before, during or after the completion of a task. What tends to be more difficult to determine is:

- What skills did learners use?
- How did learners use the skills they have as they navigated their way through a task?
- Did this variability impact their acquisition of knowledge and consequently their learning outcomes?
- If so, how so?

Of course, not all stated learning intentions focus on knowledge acquisition. Some learning intentions, quite rightly, target the acquisition of what we might call 'a skill', providing even greater incentive to gain some insight into how and why learners use these skills and how we can help them to get better at doing so.

Skills and their acquisition are the subject of some debate, including whether these skills are generic, can be taught, transferred from one task to another or from one area of learning, or context, to different areas of learning. What is clear, and generally accepted, is that learners employ these skills as they go about trying to learn and they employ them in conjunction with the knowledge they have in any given content area. It really doesn't matter what we call them. As long as we can accurately identify what skills learners are using, how they are using them and why they are using them in that way and how that impacts on their learning outcomes. Then we are in a position to provide feedback to both the learners and the educators to help learners get better at learning. We can do all of these things through LPA.

Below are two examples showing how learners use these skills, one from a Year 6 student in Visual Arts (Figure 3.1) and the other from a post-graduate medicine student in a problem-based learning (PBL) tutorial (Figure 3.2).

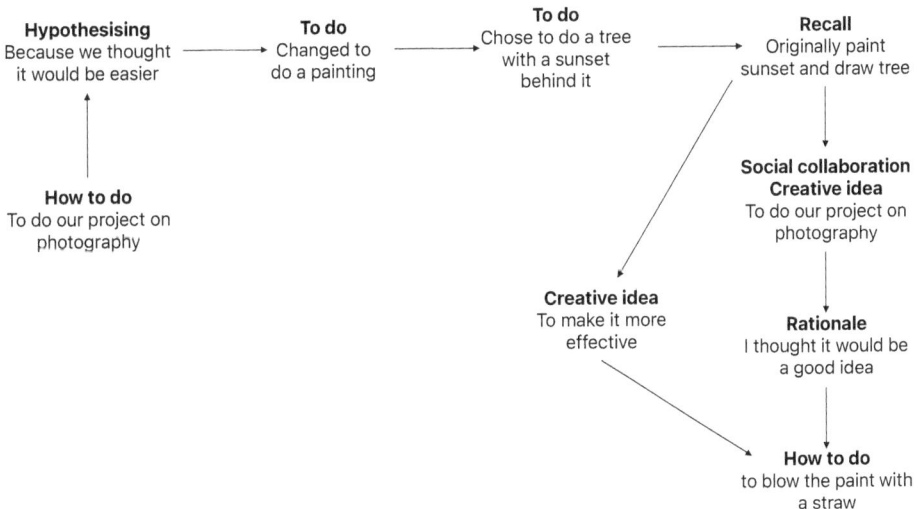

Figure 3.1: Learning process map for a grade 6 visual arts student

Description/explanation of figure 3.1: in this instance, the student is using creative skills (coming up with ideas), they are concluding and also speculating. They are also making decisions about what they are going to do and they have reasons for doing so, which are available via the learning process map.

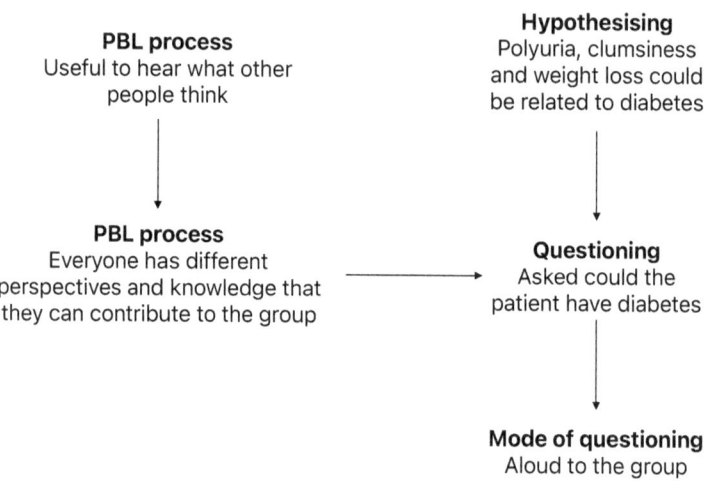

Figure 3.2: Learning process map for a post-graduate medical student in a problem-based learning tutorial

Description/explanation of figure 3.2: here we have a student using a number of well-known skills. The student is hypothesising and is also collaborating: a skill that is increasingly sought by business, with the expectation that educational institutions will develop these skills in students. I address this area of skills in chapter six. For the moment it is sufficient to see that learning process analysis can reveal students' collaboration and that they engage in hypothesising and this information can be fed back to either the student or the educator.

Learning process analysis will be described and explained in detail throughout the following sections of this book, including how to collect the relevant information (learners' decisions and their reasons for those decisions), develop learning process maps, how to interpret them and make the best use of them so that you can help learners get better at learning. The next chapter, the underlying principles upon which learning process analysis relies, lays out the foundation for applying learning process analysis.

CHAPTER FOUR

The underlying principles of learning process analysis

Using learning process analysis to make sense of what learners are doing as they go about trying to learn is based upon two principles that have been verified by research started in 1996, when I began thinking about a research program for my PhD.

Principle 1

- Learners make conscious and deliberate decisions about what they do.

Principle 2

- Learners have reasons why they make these decisions.

It is important to note that these two principles operate when students are given the opportunity to make decisions. In most learning environments, that opportunity makes up a significant portion of their learning time.

So, how do these two principles play out in the learning environment?

When learners are learning they are making conscious and deliberate decisions. These decisions will depend on the nature of the task and/or the learning environment in which they are placed. The more open the task or learning environment, the greater the choice and consequently, the more decisions made by students. These decisions are about what to do, how to do that, in addition to where to do that and when to make their decisions. This overarching principle—that learners make conscious and deliberate decisions—underpins and is the primary basis for learning process analysis.

Categories of decisions

This propensity of learners to make decisions about how they approach their learning may be categorised as follows. Learners engage in decision-making about:

- what to do (x);
- how to do x;
- when to do x; and/or
- where to do x.

These four categories in decision-making in learning may be abbreviated to:

- a decision to do (what); and then subsequently a decision about:
- how to do (how);
- when to do (when); and
- where to do (where).

Decisions result in other decisions

Each of these four categories in decision-making have defining characteristics. One of these characteristics is that the decision 'to do' tends to act as a prerequisite decision for the other three categories. Looking at the example below, the decision to 'source' is a prerequisite for the next decision about how to do so (see Figure 4.1). In this instance the decision 'when to do' was not asked. You might be able to infer 'when' (e.g. straightaway) but there are two problems with that: firstly, we do not know for sure that it occurred straight away; and secondly, it is not what learning process analysis is about. There are many methods that work on inference (i.e. we think this is what the student thought and why) and learning process analysis is designed to go beyond the imagined, to the reality of learners' decisions and why they make them. That is, LPA is a method that can microanalyse how learners approach learning.

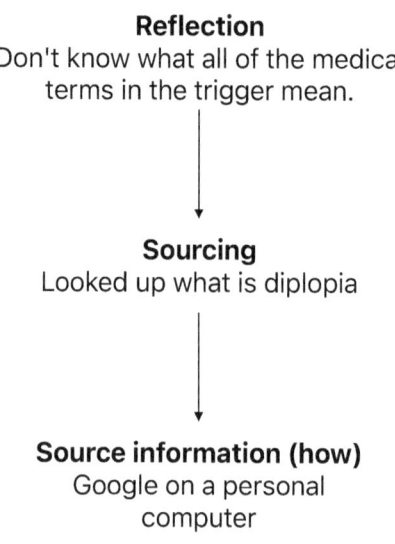

Figure 4.1: Decisions as prerequisites

Don't expect to see all types of decision-making in every learning episode as learners' decision-making is dependent on the nature of the task and/or learning environment (and maybe the questions asked by an interviewer too). The number of things learners can, and do, make decisions about, in the normal course of learning, is limitless and often idiosyncratic to each learner. This includes decisions such as deciding to collaborate, share a resource, to ask a question, to take notes, to listen to a colleague, to stay silent and to seek feedback.

The following example is designed to illustrate this aspect of learners' decisions revealed by learning process analysis. In this example only the decisions are included. In the next section, the reasons for these decisions, which illustrate the second underlying principle, are described and discussed.

Shane is a junior high school student undertaking a science field trip at a local field studies centre. When given the task of investigating how plants and animals interact with each other at a field study centre, Shane makes a decision to use a dip net. Shane also decides which part of the pond they are going to dip the net. Shane also decides where to place the dip net and how to use the dip net. Shane's specific decisions are to:

- use a dip net (what);
- use the dip net at the edge of the pond (where);
- place the dip net near the bottom of the pond (where); and
- move the dip net about and swish it back and forth at the bottom of the pond (how).

That precursory decision is to use a dip net. The remaining decisions do not occur if this initial decision (what to do) is not made.

This example also illustrates the first principle underlying learning process analysis: that learners make conscious decisions about how they approach their learning. All of the decisions made by learners and shown in these learning process maps are conscious and deliberate. That is, they do not just happen.

Decisions are underpinned by reasons

The second underlying principle of learning process analysis is that when students make decisions about learning, they have reasons for doing so. The learner in the above example has made the decisions set out above and has reasons for making each decision. The decisions and reasons are set out below:

Reason: (because I) wanted to catch something.

Decision: (I decided) to use a dip net;

Reason: (and because I) 'hadn't been there and wanted to see what was there' (two reasons really)

Decision: (I decided) to use the dip net at the edge of the pond;

Reason: (and because I) 'thought they'd all be the same'

Decision: (I decided) to place the dip net near the bottom of the pond; and

Reason: (and because I) 'thought it might help to get more animals'

Decision: (I decided) to move the dip net about and swish it back and forth at the bottom of the pond.

The resultant learning process map is below (Figure 4.2).

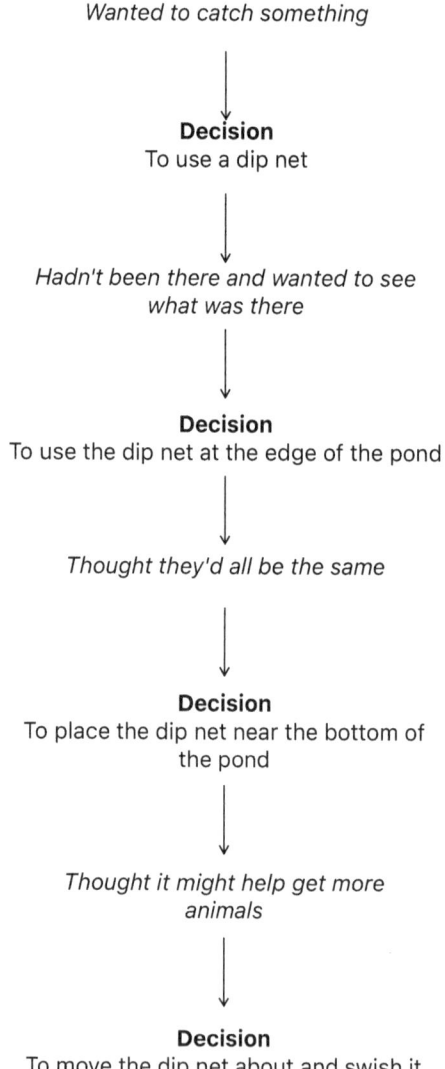

Figure 4.2: *Learning process map showing decisions and reasons why*

As I hope you will see later in this book, having access to the decision-making of learners provides significant and detailed insight into how learners approach their learning. Consequently, learning process analysis has huge advantages in providing specific and detailed feedback to learners in order to help them get better at learning (see figure 4.3).

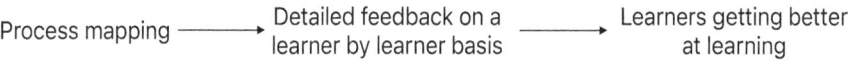

Figure 4.3: The role that learning process analysis can play

It might be tempting to dismiss this combination of decision-making + reasons as fairly trivial, maybe even inconsequential. However, for learners, this combination of making decisions and having reasons for these decisions is anything but trivial. For learners, this combination is critical to their success in the business of learning. For learners this is the main game. In short, this series of decisions and reasons is how learners learn.

The reality is that how learners approach their learning is idiosyncratic, messy, complex and difficult to assess. When you multiply those characteristics of learning by thirty or so learners, unravelling and genuinely helping all learners to the best of your ability is a difficult and demanding, sometimes never-ending, task. And that would be under the best of conditions. Learning process analysis enables detailed access to this complexity facilitating targeted and detailed feedback to individual learners.

Problem Based Learning

PBL is used worldwide in education, mainly though not exclusively, in post-secondary education and in many medical schools. I will spend a little time below describing what PBL is and how it plays out in the context of a medical school, mainly because some of the terms are peculiar to medical schools. Problem-based learning varies in its implementation from one facility to another. It generally comprises small groups working on a patient-based problem over several sessions. These sessions may be spread over three separate days, two days or completed in one day and can be managed in-person or online. Typically, a PBL tutor would be present to facilitate the session.

The first thing a student in a PBL tutorial sees is a short description of how a person presents (how they are feeling, symptoms, some character description and background narrative) sometimes called 'the trigger'. From the trigger, students identify relevant information and any unfamiliar terms and formulate the nature of the problem as best they can in the form of a problem statement. They then brainstorm and generate tentative hypotheses and identify learning issues for further study which they will report back on at a subsequent tutorial. Multiple iterations of these steps may occur over the course of a single problem.

This partly-managed learning environment is designed to help a group of learners interact socially and academically. We will explore how the two underlying principles of learning process analysis can help us to make sense of what is happening in PBL sessions.

The principles of learning process analysis and PBL

I'd like to briefly describe what learning process analysis can show us using some examples from PBL and illustrate how these two underlying principles provide the insight we gain from learning process analysis. The first example is from the initial PBL tutorial session when the patient presentation is provided to the students.

The contributing of questions relating to the trigger, as done by this learner, is exactly the sort of response expected of a student in a PBL session. Also, and again as you might expect in any small group working environment, the questions are asked aloud to the group. Many institutions offering PBL also tend to use online learning management systems, hence the student typing directly in the shared file (which would either be visible on a screen (in-person) or a shared screen (online).

THE UNDERLYING PRINCIPLES OF LEARNING PROCESS ANALYSIS

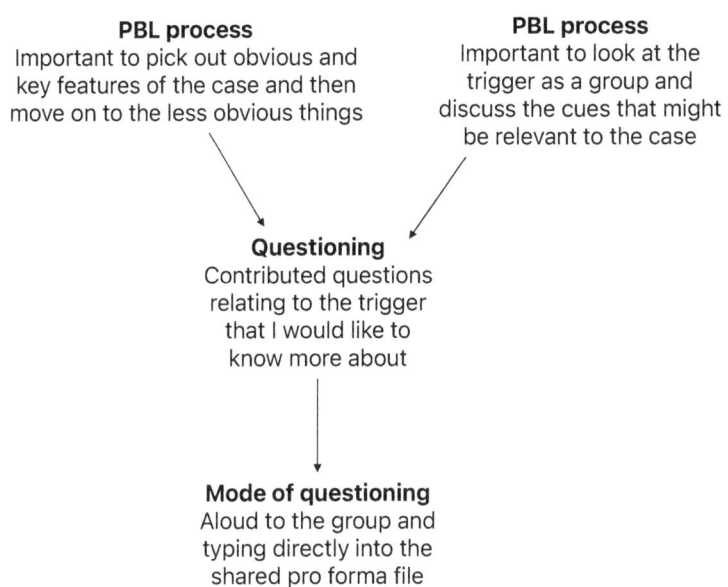

Figure 4.4: Learning process map of a student for session 1 (out of 3) in a medical problem-based learning session

The student's decision-making (commenting and how they did so) are readily observed by anyone with access to the PBL session (sitting in the room, audio recording, videorecording, online guest etc). What learning process analysis provides is access to this decision-making and validates that the learner has made a series of conscious decisions. Learning process analysis also provides access to the reasoning for the decision-making. In this instance they had two reasons for asking their questions about the trigger. Both reasons highlight two approaches to learning that PBL is designed to promote:

- identifying key features (cues) from the patient presentation (we want students to do that in PBL); and
- the socio-constructive aspects of PBL where students are working collaboratively on the problem at hand (again, something we want students to do in any group work not just PBL—to collaborate).

Figure 4.5 shows this differentiation between what is readily observed and what is revealed when we use learning process analysis.

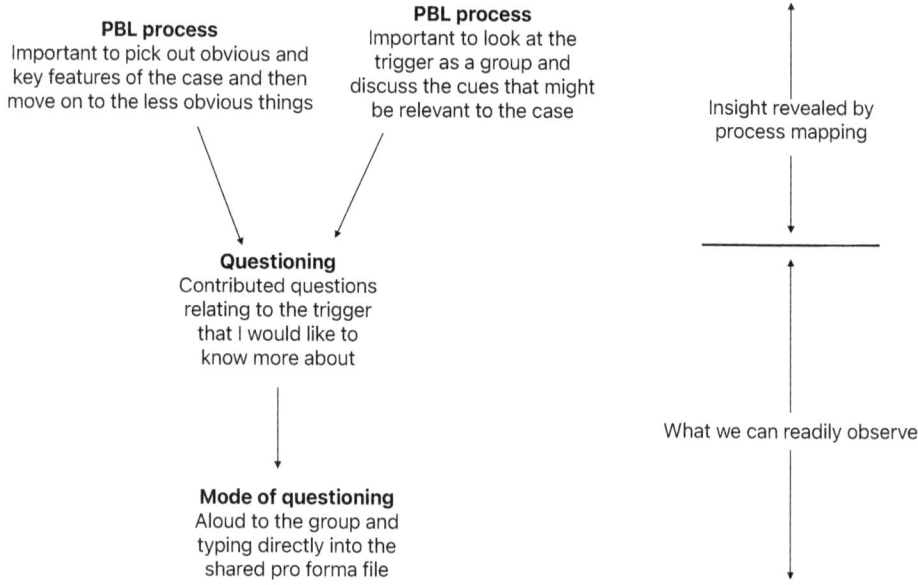

Figure 4.5: Highlighting part of the value of learning process analysis

You will see multiple examples of this sort of decision-making plus reasons throughout this book, further illustrating the underlying principles of learning process analysis and the insights it provides into how learners approach their learning.

When we develop learning environments like problem-based learning, or set up small group learning in our classes, we do so in the hope that students will be actively engaged for reasons like those above (figure 4.5). What learning process analysis does is provide clear evidence these things are happening (active learning and collaboration) and which learners are engaged and which ones are not (and importantly, why). Having access to this information enables us to help learners get better at learning by identifying areas for improvement and then working with the learners who may require additional support so they can maximise their opportunities for learning.

THE UNDERLYING PRINCIPLES OF LEARNING PROCESS ANALYSIS

Figure 4.6: For learner C in a PBL session

The example above (Figure 4.6) of C and their decision-making illustrates how she approaches her learning, at least in this instance. It is important to appreciate that C or any other learner doesn't always use the same approach. If anything, my research and the examples used in this book show that the opposite is true—that learners adapt and use a range of approaches according to need. There is probably nothing surprising or new in that statement. What is new is that learning process analysis can reveal the details of these approaches to learning, learner by learner and task by task.

One thing worth noting is that from an observational viewpoint what you observe is a student (e.g. figure 4.6) on a device (laptop ... tablet). And that is it really. You don't really know if they are engaged with the task or not. You hope they are (because that was always your intention) and you wouldn't normally explore the degree to which they are engaged, unless you were concerned about progress of the group or student. What is revealed through learning process analysis is that C is very much engaged in learning that is relevant to the problem at hand. Biggs[14], in his discussion of a cognitive systems approach to understanding learning has shown that focusing on meaning is a characteristic of deep learning. In this instance, I think it is fair to say that because we have the evidence from learning process analysis, C is focused on meaning and therefore, is engaged in deep learning. Most times, we hope these things are happening. With learning process analysis, we know they are and by whom, how so, when, to what degree and how often.

---

[14] Biggs, J. (1993). From theory to practice: A cognitive systems approach. Higher Education Research and Development, 12, 73-86.

One of the original design intentions of problem-based learning, and there were many, was that it would nudge[15] learners towards recognising what they do or don't know and that if they encounter something they do not know or understand that they should follow-up on that. C is doing exactly that by following up on their recognition of not understanding a term, so they were better positioned to make sense of the patient presentation. For those unfamiliar with PBL as it is most commonly practised, the role of the PBL tutor is not to provide answers to questions. That is, the tutor is not there as a content expert. Their role is to manage the group's collective meanderings towards a considered and targeted management plan for the patient, based on the diagnosis upon which the group agrees (or at least reaches consensus on). The original developers of PBL in medical schools at McMaster University would be pleased to see such clear evidence of PBL moving learners towards recognition of prior learning, working out what they do or don't know, what they need to know and then acting on that recognition.

One of the things that happens in the problem-based learning environment is that information can be selectively released to students at specific points in the problem. The example below (see Figure 4.7) shows the decision-making of a PBL student in the second session of a PBL problem, after the patient history has been made available to the group. Sometimes this information is extracted by role play, with one learner playing the role of a medical student or doctor and another student assuming the role of the patient. This is generally known as 'taking a history'—you might notice your doctor doing that occasionally.

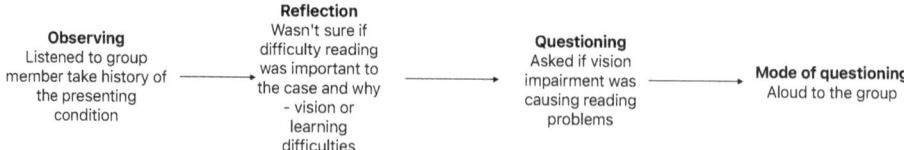

Figure 4.7: Decision-making in session 2 of a PBL problem

---

[15] If you wish to further explore the concept of nudging, I recommend you read Sunstein, CR and Thaler, RH's book, Nudge: Improving Decisions About Health, Wealth and Happiness. Penguin. 2009

D's decision was to ask about the patient's vision impairment and whether it was causing them reading problems, and she asked her question to the group members as a whole (i.e. to no-one in particular). This example is similar, and also different to, the decision-making of C just above. In D's instance, the decision to ask the question stemmed not from a misunderstanding of a term as with C but related more to the processes of clinical reasoning. It still shows a student unsure but in this instance, about the relevance of some of the patient history to understanding the possible cause of the patient's presentation. In D's example the reasons (i.e. the second underlying principle of learning process analysis) provide this insight about D's thinking, in particular their clinical reasoning. This reflection by the student about the patient's difficulty with reading is also something PBL is designed to elicit from students. I hope you can begin to see that gaining access to a student's decision-making, including their reasons for any decision-making, provides real insight into their approach to learning whether that be in PBL or any other learning environment.

The importance of the two principles of learning process analysis

It is easy to miss the importance of these two underlying principles of learning process analysis. Students are constantly making decisions about what they are going to do, how they do so, sometimes when and where they do so. They will always have reasons for their decision-making. These underlying principles feed into the construction of learning process maps with the result that we have real insight into what learners are doing and why. That is, how they are learning to know.

These principles apply to all learners and all areas of learning. Take the following example which is of an 11-year-old student working on an art project of their choice (see Figure 4.8). E is a primary student who was tasked with creating an art project. Time was available every day to work on the project. The project was a joint project with E working collaboratively with F, another student in the same class. So, what does E's learning process map tell us? The decision to draw the artwork was made for a fairly straightforward and expedient reason—she wasn't the best at painting and for that reason made the decision to draw. I will briefly touch on one aspect of learning process analysis here which will be discussed more thoroughly in chapters 5 and 6. It is important not to infer too much from this decision + reason. So, although E is not the best at painting, we don't have any information to suggest that E thought she was better at drawing.

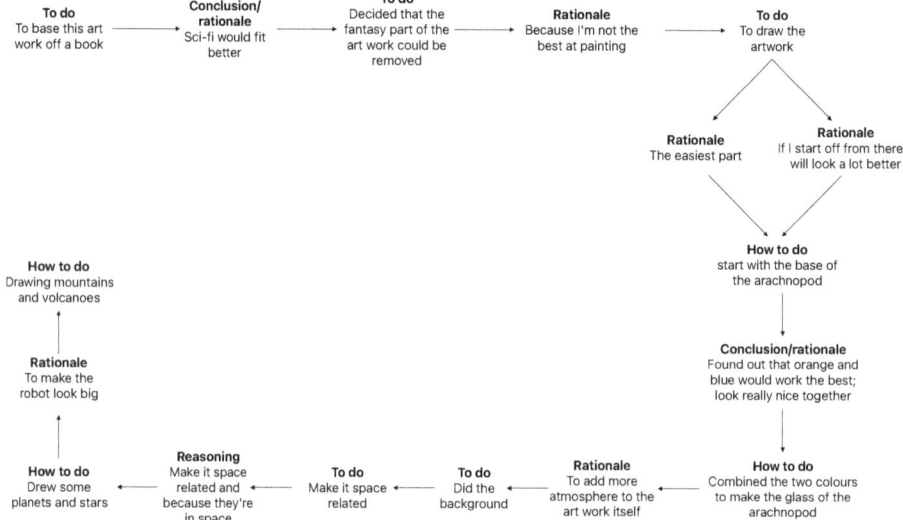

Figure 4.8: Learning process map of a student undertaking an art project

I have shared this example, in addition to the PBL learning process map above, to illustrate that the two underlying principles of learning process analysis apply to learners of all ages in any area of learning. In the second part of E's learning process map we gain a little more insight into her reasoning. One reason she made the decision to start with the base of the arachnopod[16] was similar, though not identical to the initial reason for drawing not painting. E thought that starting with the base was going to be easier. Her other reason for starting with the base is more closely

---

[16] If you are unsure what an arachnopod is, please see https://amulet.fandom.com/wiki/Arachnopod

related to her thinking about this project, in that she thought the drawing would look better if they started it this way. If we are to gain insight into how learners approach their learning so that we can help them get better at learning it is insights such as these, courtesy of learning process analysis that will facilitate that goal.

An additional feature of learning process analysis is that it can be used for an assessment of curriculum requirements. A typical curriculum requirement in junior art might be something along the lines, 'students are able to explain how ideas are represented in artworks' (taken from the national curriculum in Australia). There are several instances where E describes their ideas:

- 'to add more atmosphere to the artwork …' is behind the decision to 'make it space related'; and
- 'to make the robot look big' by 'drawing mountains and volcanoes'.

Whether learners are successful or unsuccessful, engaged or disengaged in their learning, are online or in-person, engaged in a simulation activity or creating an artwork, they are making decisions and these decisions are about how they engage in the business of learning. Typically, and in all learning environments, learners will make decisions about the following:

- to source information (e.g. 'looked up the meaning of diplopia');
- how to source that information (e.g. 'the internet');
- to question (e.g. 'asked about visual fields');
- how to question (e.g. 'aloud to the group');
- to reflect (e.g. 'confused about a concept presented in the case and could sense that other people were confused as well');
- To comment (e.g. 'shared information with the group').
- to integrate prior knowledge (e.g. 'remembered learning about cranial nerves but couldn't remember detail');
- to collaborate (e.g. listened to a colleague present a post on areas of pituitary and hormones involved);
- to design an investigation;

- to observe;
- to hypothesise;
- to conclude;
- to state results;
- to share results;
- to control variables;
- to predict;
- to communicate;
- to stay silent;
- to classify;
- to compare data;
- to record results;
- to record conclusions; and
- to analyse data, as some examples.

In the context of school learning, the learner might be researching some homework for school. As part of that research process a learner may make a decision about how to make sense of the topic they have been asked to research, or which topic they will research. If they choose (i.e. decided) to research a topic, they have made a decision about that and they will have a reason, or reasons, for that decision. Once the topic is decided upon, decisions will be made about how to go about making sense of the topic and refining the topic into component parts so the learner may make sense of it. The decisions here are what to do and then how to do it—and for each of these decisions they will have reasons. They will also make conscious decisions about how long to spend on the research and how to break that time up. They will make decisions, for particular reasons, about how to research their topic and if searching on the internet, what terms to search, which webpages to read, whether to gather and then read later and so on.

Learners will have different reasons for the same decision (a case study)

The vagaries of what might seem a simple decision and the intricate nature of the decision-making process is best illustrated by a series of learning process maps from Figure 4.9a through to 4.9g. These maps are presented as a mini-case study using the learning process maps and a narrative showing how learners may have very different reasons (and sometimes the same) for what appears to be a straightforward decision—'to ask a question'.

The context for this case study is problem-based learning (PBL) and is focused on one aspect of group interaction—'collaboration by asking a question'. Although these examples are taken from a medical student PBL context, the key messages also apply to any group context where 'asking a question' applies. Those other contexts might include a meeting of board directors, a work project meeting or a publisher's weekly meeting as some examples. These contexts are all typical, everyday situations in which a member of a group might decide to ask a question, either to the group as a whole or to another group member.

The examples below also show people engaging in collaboration. Collaboration is explored in considerable detail in chapter six including how learning process analysis provides insights into this desired soft skill.

This complexity of learning, revealed in the context of a simple, everyday instance also reveals both the beauty and the complexity of learning and underscores how difficult it is to help people learn effectively and efficiently.

The first two examples (4.9a and 4.9b), from the same learner, show two different reasons for the same decision (to ask a question). The questions themselves are not too dissimilar with the reasons behind the decision provide an insight into this learner's approach to learning. In Figure 4.9a the learner is using the opportunity PBL provides to potentially assist their learning. Figure 4.9b shows us that this learner is adopting one of the key approaches to PBL and to one important element of problem-based learning—clinical reasoning. The approach this learner is taking, described in just about any introduction to PBL, is to think broadly and not to rule out a possible cause before having more information. This same principle of thinking broadly might also apply in the boardroom, where thinking broadly and asking open-ended questions is a useful avenue to developing well-considered strategy and policy formation. The same approach applies to compliance, where only too often we hear about a lack of compliance via the front page of the newspaper. Thinking broadly in the boardroom and asking questions, even ones with highly improbable answers, may well have prevented some of the more memorable boardroom failures.

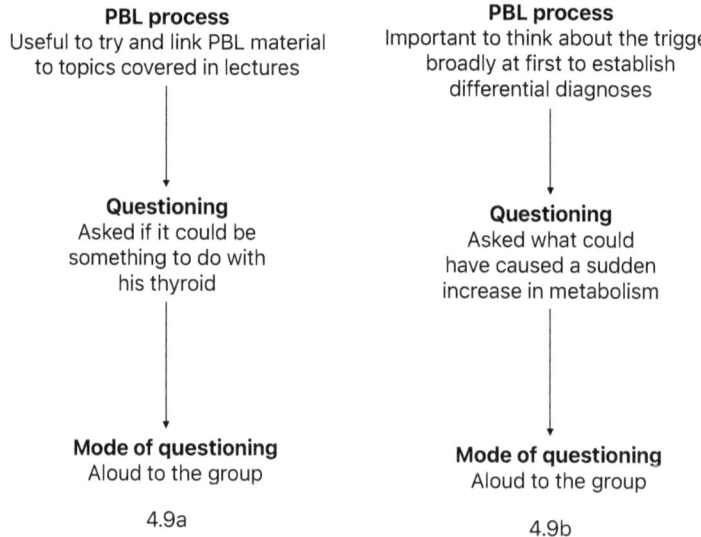

Figure 4.9a and 4.9b: Different reasons for the same decision

The next example, Figure 4.9c, highlights several features of PBL (in any context). One of those aspects is what we want students to do in PBL: gain an understanding about specific concepts. The other component is, of course, how that happens, in this case through asking a question. We also see that the learner asking the question does so to gain some clarification, which suggests this learner was seeking to better understand that 'aspect of physiology'.

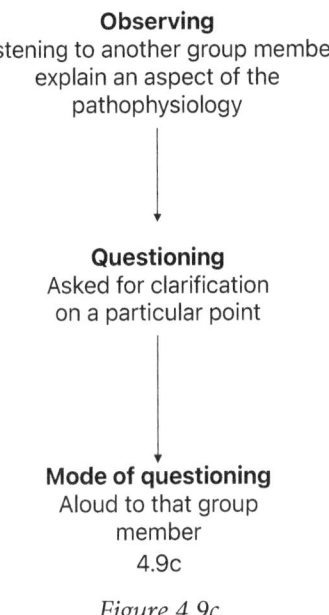

Figure 4.9c

Of course, we also need to understand how to use this information. Seeking understanding is a critical aspect of learning. In the above example we have clear evidence of the student seeking understanding. One approach to using learning process analysis to assist learning is to explore this aspect of learning amongst a group of learners. If, over time, we can see evidence of a student who is not 'seeking understanding' and if that were correlated with poor assessment results, we have a potential avenue to helping a student not just to get better at learning but also to achieve better learning outcomes.

If we take this scenario out of the classroom and into another context such as a boardroom with directors attending to the agenda of the day, we can also apply learning process analysis to understanding how people contribute to the group. It is important to remember, particularly in the context of a boardroom, that learning process analysis is a descriptive process and is used for reviewing what happened and is not prescriptive, suggesting how, when or why to do something. Back to the boardroom—one approach for LPA in the boardroom is to use it as an auditing tool. Why was that decision made? Who contributed to the discussion? Who asked questions? Why were those questions asked? Who didn't? Are there some board members who ask questions more than others? Are there some directors who just don't ask questions? Why is that the case? And it is in the 'why' that the real analysis take place. There is nothing inherently wrong in not asking questions, particularly if there is no need and the person made that decision to enable others to contribute to the discussion or because they thought the people asking questions were asking the same questions they were thinking of. Learning process analysis peels back the layers behind the observable and enables this type of analysis—no matter the context.

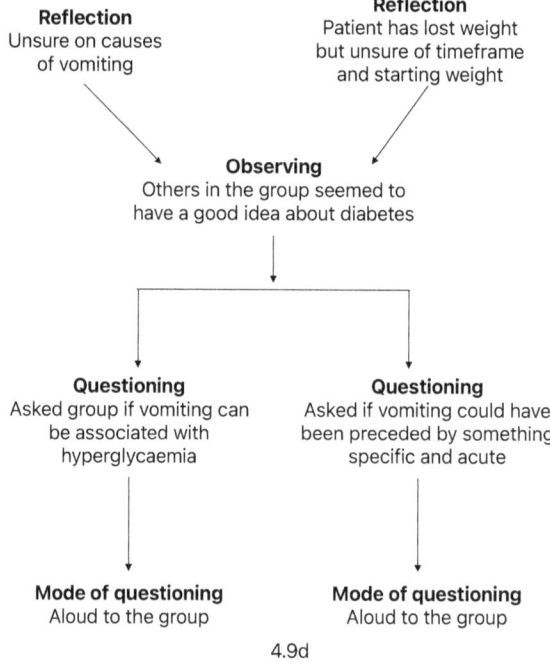

Figure 4.9d

Figure 4.9d shows a learner unsure about something and aware others in the group have knowledge she does not have and for those reasons asks two questions to the group at large. The same principle applies to Figures 4.9e – 4.9g, using the group to be efficient rather than remain ignorant—useful lessons that can apply across any context.

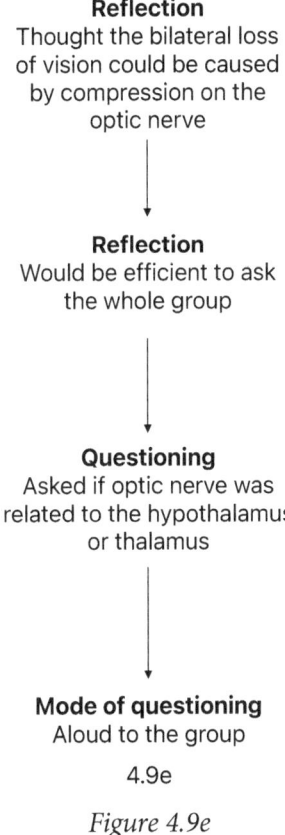

Figure 4.9e

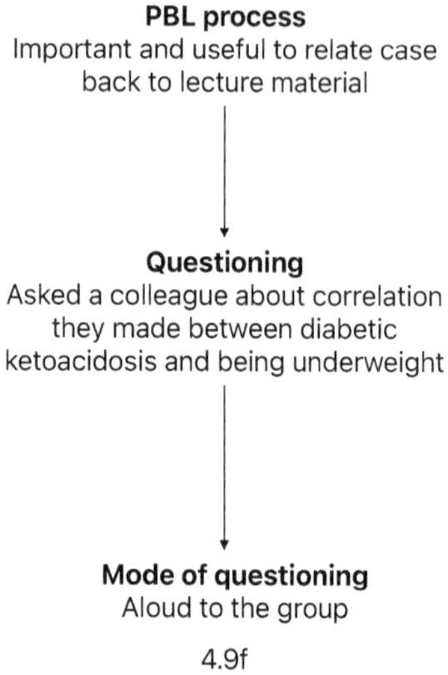

PBL process
Important and useful to relate case
back to lecture material

↓

Questioning
Asked a colleague about correlation
they made between diabetic
ketoacidosis and being underweight

↓

Mode of questioning
Aloud to the group

4.9f

Figure 4.9f

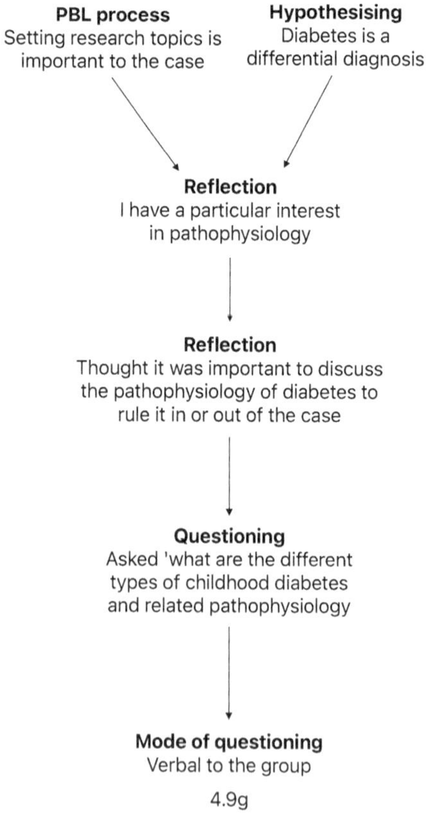

PBL process　　　　**Hypothesising**
Setting research topics is　　Diabetes is a
important to the case　　differential diagnosis

↘　　　↙

Reflection
I have a particular interest
in pathophysiology

↓

Reflection
Thought it was important to discuss
the pathophysiology of diabetes to
rule it in or out of the case

↓

Questioning
Asked 'what are the different
types of childhood diabetes
and related pathophysiology

↓

Mode of questioning
Verbal to the group

4.9g

Figure 4.9g

In summary—decisions are made for reasons, always

The reasons for making decisions about learning may be quite varied. People will make different decisions because one day they are hungry and on another they are not, because they had a disagreement with their parent, their caregiver, their sister, brother, friend, their colleague at work, because they think the chair of the board should be someone else, maybe even them. They will make different decisions based on what they know or what they don't know (as we saw above) about a particular topic. They will make different decisions depending on their skill set (say in art for instance, or a recreated drama, or a board member without a legal or accounting background). They may make different decisions based on their interest in an area and this list is potentially infinite and that is why we need a method that can forensically examine the decision-making of learners and provide detailed clarity about how they approach their learning.

CHAPTER FIVE

Insights from research that inform learning process analysis

As described in the previous chapter, learning process analysis is reliant upon two principles verified by research spanning twenty-five years:

1. learners make conscious and deliberate decisions about what they do; and
2. learners have reasons why they make these decisions.

These principles operate when students are given the opportunity to make decisions, which, in learning environments, is a significant portion of the time students spend engaged in the business of learning. I used several examples to illustrate these principles and how they underpin learning process analysis.

Research insights into learning process analysis

Following on from these two principles of learning process analysis are additional research-verified findings which support its use as a method that can help us better understand learning. These research-verified findings may be summarised as follows:

1. The precise nature of learners' decisions can be extracted, mapped and categorised.
2. Most people have very little insight into their decision-making processes.

3. Feedback to learners about their decision-making can lead to improved learning outcomes.

Using the methods described in this book you can identify learners' decisions and their reasons for these decisions in significant detail. With the detailed accurate data that learning process analysis provides, we can classify the types of decisions made.

The precise nature of learners' decision-making can be extracted, mapped and categorised

One of the features of learning process analysis is that the maps provide feedback previously unavailable to learners. The methods currently used to extract decision-making and reasons in order to construct learning process maps are displayed in figure 5.1 below.

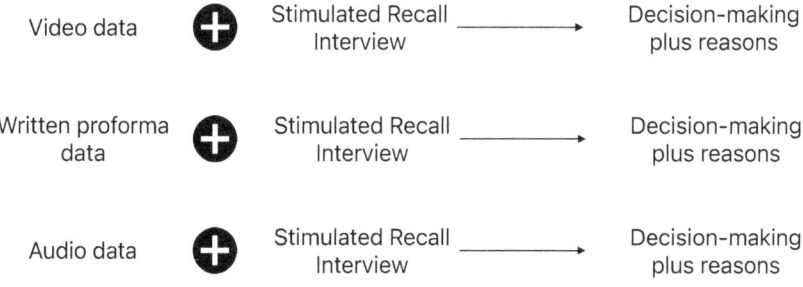

Figure 5.1: The three main methods for extracting learners' decisions and reasons

I will now touch briefly on these methods, which are comprehensively described in chapter seven. The first step is for learners' decision-making to be captured in some way. Currently, that is done using video data, written proforma or audio data. This initial step provides learners' basic decision-making data which is converted to text.

The second step uses the information from step 1 and explores it in more detail by drilling down into the learner's decision-making and reasons, diving down into *why* decisions were made by the learner. This second step is known as **stimulated recall interviewing**. Stimulated recall interviewing (SRI) uses data captured by other means (such as the proforma referred to above) as a prompt to guide questioning of the decisions participants make. SRI has been used successfully to gather accurate data in a range of health education and education settings. During a stimulated recall interview learners are asked whether they made a conscious decision about an instance, and if so, what that decision was. As each decision or action is described, participants are probed further to ascertain the underlying reasons for those decisions. As a microanalytic method, SRI is very well suited to determining what learners are doing when going about the business of learning.

Insights into decision-making about learning

Learners tend to have little insight into their decision-making processes as they go about the business of learning. This observation should not come as too much of a surprise. Most learners just 'do'—that is, they go about a task or contribute to a small group, or any other activity associated with learning, in whatever way they can or wish to. As a result, what learners are doing (and especially why) tends to be implicit or unstated. What learning process analysis does is make explicit these hidden aspects of learning. The following examples of a small-group tutorial illustrate the explicit details delivered via learning process analysis (see Figure 5.2).

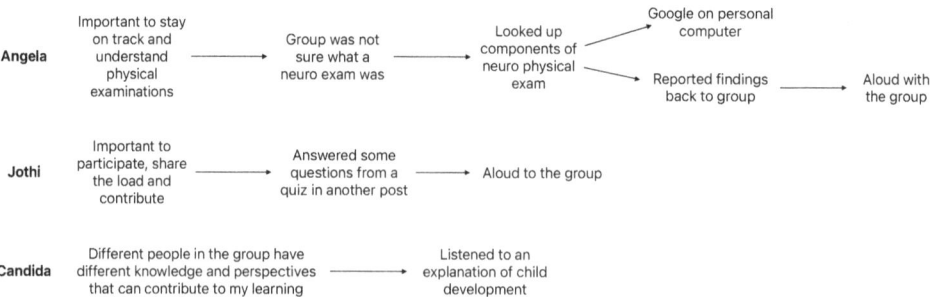

Figure 5.2: Revealing the implicit via LPA

If we were watching Angela, we would have observed her report back to the group and if we had access to Angela's device, we could determine exactly what was looked up and how. The insight we gain using learning process analysis is why Angela made the decisions she did. It is this information about 'why' that opens a door to understanding Angela's approach to learning. Angela is being a collaborative group member, contributing to the group and is doing so for what would be seen as all the right reasons. In this context, a first-year medical student in a PBL group, staying on track and understanding physical examination data are key parts of their learning journey. This is exactly the sort of decision-making the developers of PBL were hoping students would use.

You wouldn't expect to see much from just one learning process map and any insight, such as that above, is limited. With a collection of learning process maps, potentially taken at different time intervals, we are better placed to make inferences about a student's approach to learning. These aspects and others that relate to the effective use of learning process analysis will be described and discussed in more detail in chapter seven.

In Jothi's learning process map, once again, we see that he answered some questions and did so to the group. And again, the insight gained via learning process analysis is why Jothi did what he did. In other words, why he thinks it is important to participate, to share the load and to contribute. This might seem a bit simple and a bit obvious but once we start to explore these insights in more detail, and with more data as we do in the next two chapters, I hope you will see how learning process analysis can assist us in helping learners to get better at learning.

These insights can flow in several directions. They can inform us about how students approach their learning. They can shed light on how a group is functioning and the contributions of individual students. They can be used to provide feedback to both the student and their teacher. They can also be used to understand how learners go about approaching learning from a research perspective. All of these aspects will be explored in the next chapter.

Feedback to learners about their decision-making can assist in achieving improved learning outcomes.

One of the often-stated goals of learning is for learners to be able to self-regulate their learning (often referred to as self-regulated learning). Another, similar and different goal, is for learners to be able to direct their learning (called self-directed learning).

The key to achieving better learning outcomes is to make decisions that produce better outcomes and to make those decisions more often. To do that we need to understand what decisions people make, why they make these decisions and to use that information to address and improve their learning.

CHAPTER SIX

Using learning process maps to get better

Introduction

When people make decisions that have poor outcomes, it doesn't necessarily mean they are a poor decision maker. It may be that they are making these decisions because of a lack of knowledge about a particular aspect, or a specific skill deficit, and it is these elements that impact their decision-making. By unpacking an individual's decision-making, learning process analysis will reveal why individuals are making these decisions and achieving poor outcomes. With access to this information interventions can be developed, whether skill-based or knowledge-based, and learners' outcomes can be consistently improved.

In education you might typically hear the following:

'As a learner, I want to be able to get accurate and precise feedback about how I learn in order to get better results.'

'As a teacher, I want to be able to get detailed feedback about how my learners learn in order to help them get better at learning.'

'As a learning organisation, I want to be able to provide learners with a tool that gives them accurate and precise feedback about how they learn in order to give our students the best opportunity to learn from us.'

The name of the game in educational contexts is learning. That's it. All educators at all levels of learning have an expectation that their students will learn. There is also a growing interest in wanting to help learners to be more knowledgeable about how to learn and to self-regulate their learning. Self-regulating learners tend to be more active participants in their learning. To get learners to that point they need to have insight into how they go about learning and whether they regulate how they learn and why they do so. Learning process analysis can provide forensic-level detail about how each learner goes about their learning and help move students to a more independent, self-regulating approach.

Learning process analysis is highly practical, implementable and provides almost immediate results. It can provide insight to teachers about which learners need greater input from them and which learners can be left to work more independently, knowing they have the skills and a more complete toolkit of decision-making that enables them to be effective learners.

Many countries have stated positions on wanting school-aged students to become successful learners. Learning process analysis can help students achieve that goal. These same countries also express a desire for students to acquire complex skills that help students to problem solve, think critically and be creative. Again, learning process analysis can help students achieve these goals.

In his book *Visible Learning*, John Hattie ranks a number of strategies in terms of their influence on student achievement. Three of these strategies are providing formative evaluation (ranked #4), feedback (#10) and metacognitive strategies (#14). Hattie has suggested we need to move to 'how to learn' (Hattie, 2012, 103). Clearly learning process analysis can play a role in moving in this direction.

You may well have a number of questions about learning process analysis. These might include the following:

- How is this practical for me in the classroom?
- How will I, a busy classroom teacher, use learning process analysis:
  - To help students understand their learning?
  - To develop greater independence in learners?
  - To be able to drive their learning in a more independent way?

- To help students become more effective and efficient learners?
- To help learners get better at learning?
o What do I need to do?

It is my earnest intent to answer all of these questions for you and to provide you with the knowledge and skills to use learning process analysis effectively and efficiently.

As a feedback tool

There is no way we can move learners to an understanding of 'how to learn' (Hattie, 2012, 103) without feedback. LPA can play a role in helping learners to do that. As a feedback tool, learning process maps can reveal: what decisions are being made; how decisions are being made; why decisions are being made; when decisions are being made; and, of course, by whom. They can be used in any context and any content area.

Learning process analysis can identify what mistakes learners are making and why they are making mistakes, including whether it is due to a lack of content knowledge. They can assist learners and their teachers in identifying which approaches to learning work best for which learners in which context and/or content area. Do some learners approach learning in mathematics differently to how they approach literacy, or history, or science? Learning process analysis can provide answers to these questions. What we have with learning process analysis is a tool that can describe the idiosyncratic approaches learners adopt when they go about trying to learn. Learning process analysis can provide a foundation for a much more precise approach to individualising learning.

The main focus of learning process analysis as a feedback tool is the individual learner. That is where the benefit is greatest. How does a learner approach a creative project in art? How and why do they carry out an investigation in science? Are there approaches to learning that a learner isn't using which they could use? Are there cognitive skills that a learner uses in one area and not in another?

Does that matter? Is a learner's acquisition of knowledge impeded by skills not used? Measuring progress over time for an individual learner is one approach. For example, is a learner's use of cognitive skills developing a more sophisticated nature? What activities can I design that will extend the use of some cognitive skills and not others? How can I extend the cognitive skill development of an individual? Does doing so have a beneficial effect on their learning? On their acquisition of knowledge? On their capacity to solve problems in mathematics? On their ability to construct a piece of writing?

On a collective or group level, there are other avenues for the use of learning process maps. How can I design a program so that it fits with how most of the students in a class learn? Are there approaches to learning that are common to learners and which are more effective? How can I use that knowledge to group learners for particular tasks? How do I assess the productivity of a group? How can I use learning process analysis to assess the use of soft skills like communicating and collaborating? The reality of learning process analysis is that it can be used for all of these things. Knowing how learners work together in a group and how they construct learning in a shared setting is valuable knowledge which can be used to assist learners to get the most out of group work.

Learning process analysis and knowledge acquisition

Knowledge acquisition is a significant component of learning. The acquisition of knowledge, or learning, is the outcome of moving from surface knowing to deep knowing to transfer of knowledge[17]. It follows that there should be evidence of behaviours associated with these transitory phases in any process-based analysis of learning.

The characteristics of deep learning play a vital role in the construction of knowledge by learners. Multiple descriptions of learning have shown this is what learners do—they discuss, they

---

[17] Hattie & Donoghue, 2016

listen, they ask questions and they think. Learning is triggered by intrinsic motivation. So being able to detect the nature of this motivation in learners can help us to help them get better at learning.

Learners also seek meaning. That is, they relate and extend ideas, they look for patterns and underlying principles, they check evidence and relate it to conclusions/data obtained, they are constructively critical and actively interested in course content. All are characteristics of learners attempting to acquire knowledge. Being able to accurately and reliably detect all these aspects of learning through learning process analysis is a real plus in helping learners to get better at learning.

Educators sometimes refer to shallow learning versus deep learning. In order to go from shallow to deep learning a learner's knowledge structures need to be challenged. All learning relies on this dynamic of the learner recognising what they know and what they do not know and then acting on that information. If we can obtain evidence of learners being challenged in this way, we are able to say, with some confidence, that acquisition of knowledge is occurring.

Learning process analysis can reveal all of these characteristics of knowledge acquisition. It can show that learners are making sense of new ideas, or at least trying to, how they are going about doing this and why they are doing so (i.e. their motivation). How learners source information, and their motivation for doing so, at any given time is also accessible using learning process analysis.

Knowing if your learners are hypothesising, concluding, predicting, comparing data, controlling variables, integrating prior knowledge, reflecting on prior knowledge, deciding which question to ask, collaborating (and how and why), how they go about doing something such as using materials for art, to paint instead of drawing, their rationale for doing so and on what to base their investigation or activity are all elements of learning available to you through learning process analysis.

Learning process analysis enables a fine-grained form of analysis that can be done in real time, in the classroom. As a tool learning process analysis provides access to how learners use cognitive processes to acquire knowledge and how they utilise knowledge as part of their varying approaches to learning.

Self-regulated and self-directed learning

Knowing as much as possible about how your students go about their learning is something that is desirable. A good thing to have, if you like. As we move towards developing systems for supporting individualised learning, such requirements will be mandatory. We like to think that we can assist our learners to become more aware of their learning and ideally take greater charge of their learning. Two phrases that are often thrown in when discussing this aspect of learning are: self-regulated learning and self-directed learning. Unfortunately, these two different notions are used interchangeably—that is, as if they are the same thing. They are not.

Learners who **self-regulate** are aware of the goals and strategies they use to achieve and regularly monitor achievement of those goals. Learning process analysis, with its capacity to provide explicit insight into a learner's approach to learning, offers some potential here. Even if it is only used as a tool to determine whether a learner is self-regulating their learning or not and whether that approach is successful, it is worth doing.

Self-directed learning is often used alongside such terms as lifelong learning and independent learning. If we reflect on self-directed learning as a process then it is easier to see it as something that a learner engages in where learner autonomy plays a significant role. That is, the learner, for all sorts of reasons, is directing what they are learning, how they are learning and why they are learning this way. To do these things learners will make conscious decisions about what, how and why. Learning process analysis is ideally suited to provide clear and detailed feedback to learners and their teachers about how learners are engaging in self-directed learning. How then can LPA play a role?

LPA can provide accurate feedback about how learners self-regulate their learning and why they do so. Whether they regulate it to advantage (positive outcomes) or disadvantage (none, or negative, outcomes). Gaining insight into how they regulate their learning and what they are doing, and what they are not doing, can provide the basis for getting even better at regulating learning. In these ways LPA can contribute to better learning outcomes and to better self-regulation of learning.

Decision-making typically associated with self-regulated learning are learners adjusting their motivation, including aligning what they are learning with their personal interests. The following learning process maps show learners actively regulating their learning and illustrates the type of feedback these maps provide to learners.

In the first map (Figure 6.1 2A3) the learner is aligning what they are trying to learn (by listening to research posts of colleagues), with their motivation (reinforcing what is learnt in lectures). In map 2A4 the same learner has a different motivation for a different task. In addition to lecture material their motivation has two additional components: supporting other clinical skills; and gaining a better understanding of the presentation and differential diagnosis. The learning focus is about taking a history from a patient.

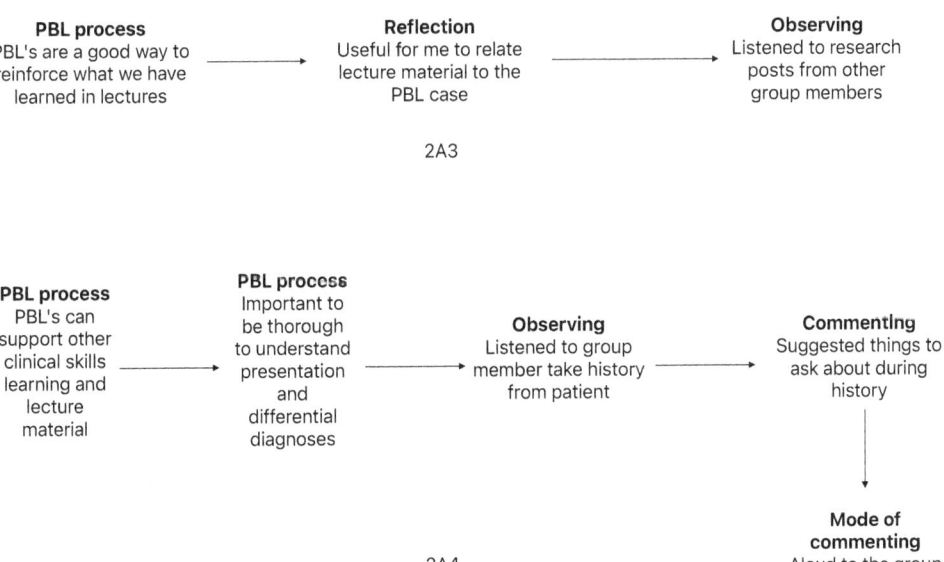

Figure 6.1: learning process analysis revealing self-regulation of learning

One practical application from this sort of data is to complete this analysis for all learners in a group and determine which of your learners are self-regulating and who is not.

LPA reveals the degree to which learners self-direct and/or self-regulate their learning. LPA also provides insight into the nature of that self-directing or self-regulating, including details of the approach a learner adopted and why they did so. The nature of the self-direction/regulation of learning can be linked to learning outcomes and provide the sort of feedback that enables a learner to modify their approach, so that it is more effective and efficient and ultimately productive.

LPA provides not just feedback to help learners get better at learning how to learn but also provides an incentive to do so. If learners can see real progress in how they approach their learning, and can see that readily, learning becomes a little easier.

Soft-skill detection

Why is this imperative for improvement so important? As outlined in the introduction, there is considerable interest in the development of soft skills, particularly in the world of work. Occupations that place an emphasis on soft skills are increasingly prevalent in the workforce and with the ongoing development of artificial intelligence and machine learning, soft skills are going to be more critical in many work environments. Soft skills, such as problem solving, collaboration, empathy and ethical behaviour, will be key accompaniments and intricately important to the effective use of artificial intelligence and machine learning.

Soft skills share many characteristics with the skills used during group work. That shared base comes from both categories of skills being related to working with others. If anything, the term 'group work' is a proxy for soft skills. The range of soft skills includes collaboration and teamwork, critical thinking, problem-solving, self-management, professional ethics, self-regulation and innovation. The next chapter describes and explores in detail the role learning process analysis can play in helping people to get better at these critical and increasingly important skills.

CHAPTER SEVEN

Real world applications of learning process analysis

Learning process analysis has much to offer beyond the typical classroom with students turning up every day to learn something. In an article examining 'lean learning' the Harvard Business Review[18] reported that throughout the world in 2016 organisations spent $359 billion (USD) on training and skills development, some of that on soft skills. The World Economic Forum lists a range of soft skills as '21st century skills'[19] and a recent report found the top three skills wanted in the workplace were soft skills[20]. As we have already seen, learning process analysis can provide insight into these in-demand soft skills for learners, employees and directors alike.

Soft skills in the workplace

Employers are increasingly requiring employees to have these soft skills, or at least be willing to acquire and develop these skills, and apply them to their day-to-day work. The same employers are placing pressure further down the line to schools and higher education, insisting they develop these skills in their students as part of their programs. Consequently, there is an expectation that soft skills will be an integral part of graduate outcomes.

---

[18] Gartner, S Where companies go wrong with learning and development October 2, 2019 Reprint HO55J1 accessed 24 June 2024.
[19] See https://www.weforum.org/agenda/2016/03/21st-century-skills-future-jobs-students/ accessed 27 June 2024
[20] See https://online.rmit.edu.au/insights/2023 accessed 24 June 2024.

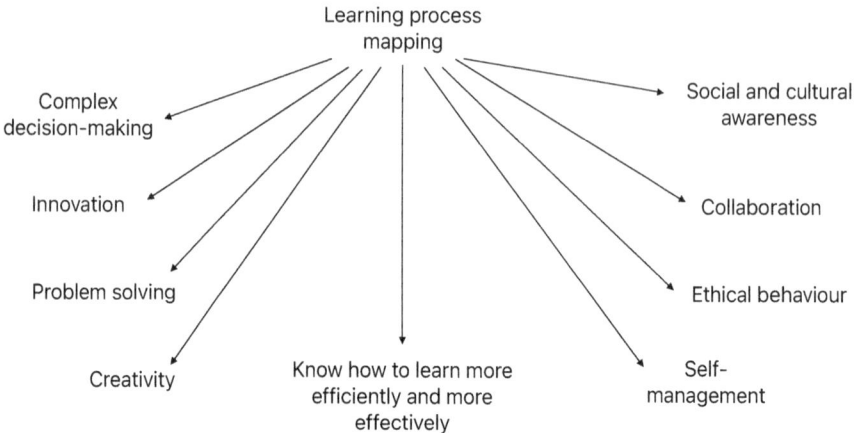

Figure 7.1: Soft skills which can be mapped and analysed by learning process analysis[21]

As illustrated in Figure 7.1 there are a range of soft skills including ethical behaviour, self-management, innovation, emotional judgement, collaboration, judgement and complex decision-making, problem solving, communication skills and an ability to learn, which learning process analysis can describe and dissect on an individual basis. I would add to this list of soft skills, 'know how to learn, more efficiently and more effectively'.

Even without the expectations of business, educational organisations see their role as helping learners acquire, develop and use these skills and get better at learning. Outcomes such as these always were in the interests of not only students but also the learning organisations. After all, who doesn't want a group of learners who collaborate, are empathetic, innovative, who can self-manage or self-regulate their decision-making about learning and who are capable of getting better at 'how to know'? Show me a learning organisation that doesn't aspire to that, either at the institutional level or at the course/subject level.

If we think more broadly about learning, developing all these skills is not just restricted to schools, colleges and universities.

---

[21] Incorporating soft skills described by Deloitte, HBR and my own research

Many other organisations are also engaged in the business of learning, whether in-house through training and development or farmed out to training organisations and consultants. As described above, a considerable sum of money is spent by business, and governments, on developing their staff. As with schools and universities, it is in the interests of all parties, employers, training organisations and those doing the learning (let's call them learners), to develop and refine these skills, including how to get better at learning, effectively and efficiently.

Mapping to assess soft skill use

In the following sections I will explore these soft skills and show how learning process analysis can play an integral role in:

- assessing how learners of all kinds, at all stages in their journeys use these skills;
- helping learners to acquire these skills;
- tracking and monitoring learners' acquisition, development and refinement of these skills; and
- certifying the acquisition and effective use of these skills.

Mapping group collaboration

When **collaboration** is examined using learning process analysis, we can see that learners make a range of decisions about how they collaborate. The result of these decisions are different ways, or types, of collaborating. In a small group, we see learners engaging with other learners in various ways. Typically, they might be asking questions of other group members; they might be nodding quietly (in agreement?). They might even be looking intensely interested and, to all intents and purposes, listening to another group member. In the workplace this soft skill might be framed as teamwork.

In just about all teaching/learning situations with small groups these and other observable actions are what we see or hear. These observable actions are what I would call our phenotypic data. Typically, such data is collected as transcripts, audio recordings or video recordings providing a combination of visual and/or oral data. Consequently, what we see as collaboration includes behaviours such as arguing and debating, describing and explaining, questioning, proposing ideas and/or solutions and, as noted above, some non-verbal behaviour such as nodding and occasionally other somewhat more expressive non-verbal behaviours.

Collaborative actions are conducive to encouraging other important actions like recognition of prior knowledge, hypothesising, reflecting and self-regulating learning.

So, what does a detailed look, using learning process analysis, reveal about how learners collaborate? We see that what we call collaboration is a range of decisions made by learners about how they engage with their colleagues during learning tasks.

In the example below (Figure 7.2) we see a learner who was listening to a colleague present something to the group (the 'post' from the group member), didn't understand something they heard, thought that a concrete example might help and so asked their colleague for clarification and did so verbally. What learning process analysis offers is the ability to go beyond the observed and explore the nature of the action in detail. What we observe is a learner asking a question of a colleague out loud. What we learn using learning process analysis is clarification of what they were thinking and the thinking behind their decision to ask a question. Learning process analysis gives us access to the reasoning for these decisions enabling us to better understand what soft skills are and how they are used.

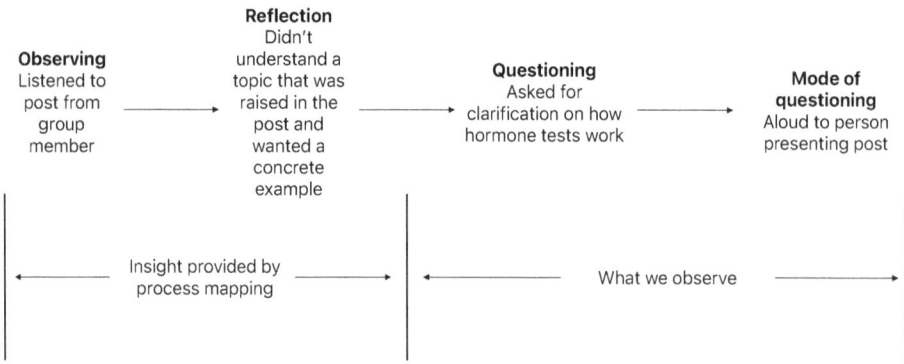

Figure 7.2: Learning process analysis revealing reasoning

In another example we see the same learner collaborating with their colleagues in a different way. On this occasion the observed action is the learner sharing some information with the group, as opposed to asking a question. The learner's reasoning, revealed by examining their decision-making and as shown in the learning process map (Figure 7.3), is different to that in Figure 7.2. Here, the learner, after listening to some of their colleagues, has looked up some items online and shared that information with the group. Part of their reasoning, and so a component of this collaborative action, is about a group working best when being collaborative and collegial and being able to trust other members of that group.

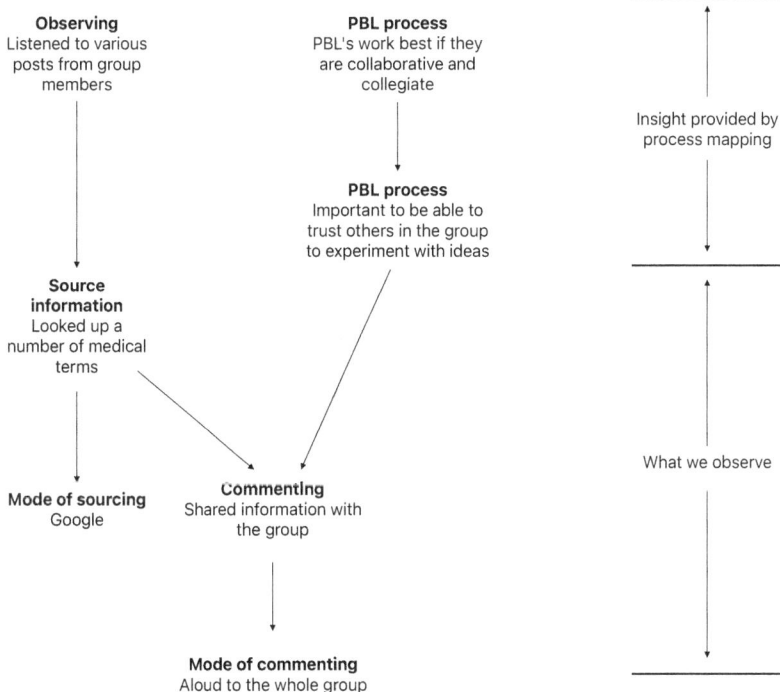

Figure 7.3: Learning process analysis revealing collaboration

These two examples show two types of collaboration. Both examples show a learner collaborating verbally with their colleagues, once as a comment and once as a question.

There are other ways of collaborating. In the following example (Figure 7.4) we have a learner deciding to collaborate by being silent and listening to their colleagues. This learner's reasoning is once again clear—to gain, potentially at least, a different perspective of the topic at hand. With this type of collaboration there is a clear motive at play. In terms of what is observable versus revealed by LPA, what we have is a student listening (at the observable level) and the rationale is to gain different perspectives. We cannot say any more than that. For instance, we cannot say that doing so will benefit the learner or even that the learner thinks it will benefit them to listen—only that they think they may gain different perspectives on 'the case'. To follow up on this, and with additional data from this learner, you could map whether this approach to listening is a consistent part of this learner's approach to working with their colleagues.

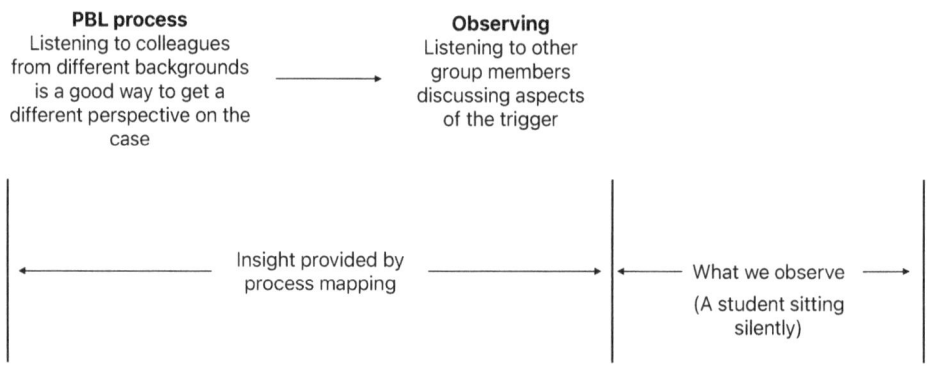

Figure 7.4: Further insight into collaboration using learning process analysis

The next example (Figure 7.5), with the same learner shows a similar, yet different rationale for why they are collaborating. In this instance, the learner is asking a question, something we would generally regard as a form of collaboration. These acts are what we expect to see in a functional small group, be that a learning group or some other group. What we gain from learning process analysis is: here is a learner actively linking what they are doing in a small group to other relevant material ('lecture'). Now we all think, or at least expect that, this is something learners might do when in a small group learning environment and here we have clear evidence that this learner is at least actively thinking about their learning.

Equally, all these finer details of collaboration can be found in the workplace or the boardroom. Take a bird's eye view of any board meeting and there will be many people listening, asking questions, contributing to the discussion and all with similar reasons—to contribute, to better understand, to actively promote collaboration amongst colleagues or to seek clarification. The key is to understand both what and why.

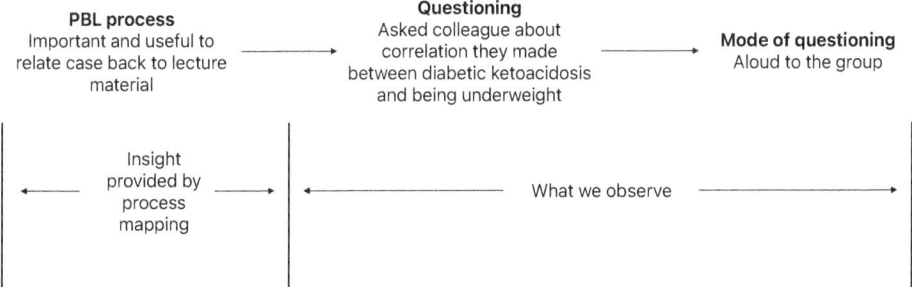

Figure 7.5: Learning process analysis providing insight into collaboration

Not all decision-making by learners about collaborating, or indeed anything else, has a rationale embedded in learning or understanding. Sometimes what we would regard as an act of collaboration ('bolding key points'—Figure 7.6) is being undertaken for no other reason than it has 'to be done'. Decision-making of this order is still collaboration and an important part of the group working well together, so we shouldn't dismiss it but we should understand why learners do things in groups and why they collaborate in certain ways. Learning process analysis can help us to do that.

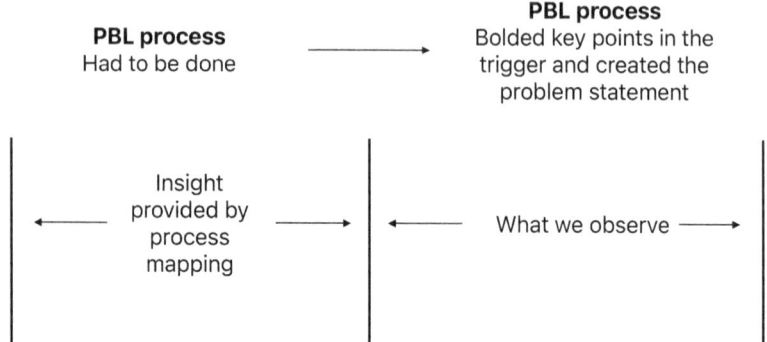

Figure 7.6: Learning process analysis revealing why learners collaborate

And sometimes collaboration takes a different form again and is very much about the group working together and maintaining positive group dynamics. In the example below (Figure 7.7) the

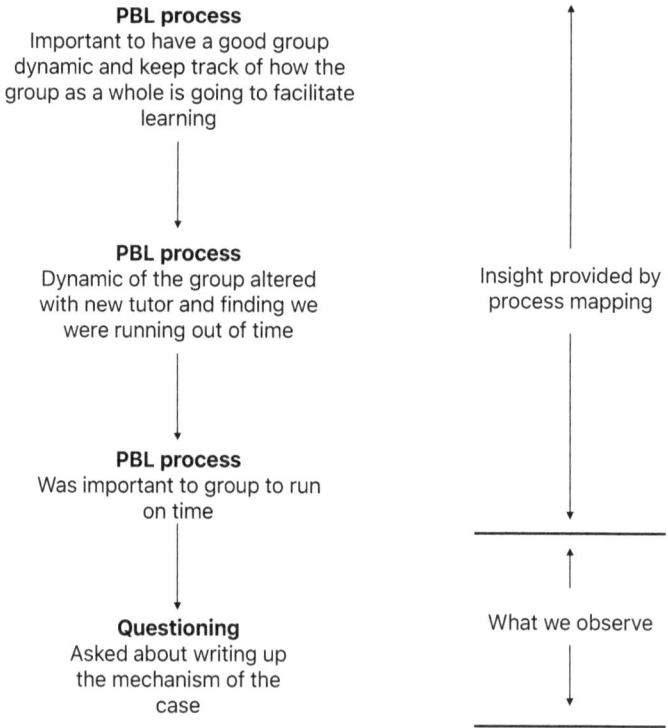

Figure 7.7: A learner actively managing group dynamics (revealed via learning process analysis)

reason for this learner's collaboration was to keep the group on time. The question, writing up the mechanism of the case, is very much a procedural step and one of the things to do as you work your way through a PBL case. The key to understanding this learning process map lies more in the reasons than in the decision itself. To facilitate productive small group learning it is very useful to know that some people keep an eye on the dynamics of the group and seek to maintain positive dynamics.

The same learner (with the same tutor as above) adopts this approach to the group at other times too. As shown in Figure 7.8 we see a learner collaborating to maintain group dynamics. The focus of this learner is to keep things 'on track'. This example highlights one of the uses of learning process analysis. Having access to a learner's decision-making and reasoning via learning process analysis enables us to identify learners who keep an eye on a group's dynamics and deliberately seek to maintain positive dynamics within a group. Not everybody does that, whether in learning or at work. It is useful to know who does and who does not.

Identifying individuals who can and do play a constructive role in managing group dynamics can assist in allocating individuals to groups and also show us the negative of this type of collaboration—those who do not engage in decision-making

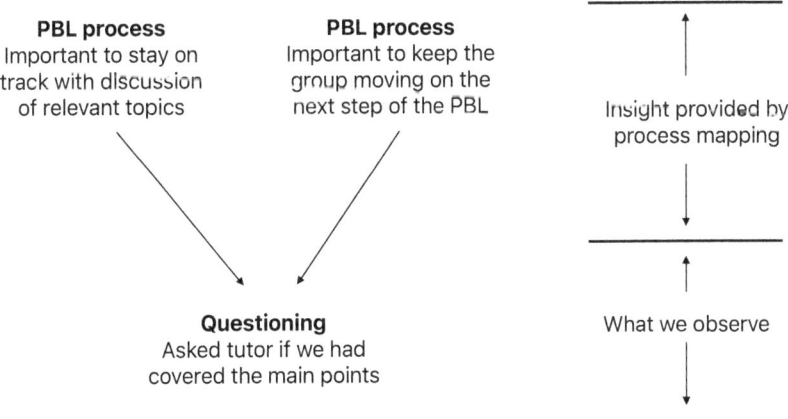

Figure 7.8: Learning process analysis identifying learners actively managing the group

about managing the group dynamics. This latter group may well play different roles and learning process analysis can assist in identifying these individuals and their roles. Some people are more inclined to share ideas and/or ask questions of their colleagues and some do all of these things (maintain group dynamics overtly, plus share ideas and ask questions).

The utility of understanding collaboration

Being able to identify how learners collaborate is only useful if we have a purpose for seeking this information. Do we want to allocate learners who tend to actively monitor group dynamics across all groups (management). Do we want to work with all learners so that as many as possible are aware of how they can contribute actively (corrective and educative). That is, do we want all learners to be able to utilise all variations of collaborating in small group work? There will be many more reasons why you might want to identify how learners collaborate. The beauty of learning process analysis is that it enables you to identify how and why learners collaborate so that you can target your efforts to particular purposes. Learning process analysis is a method that can help you help learners to keep on getting better at learning.

Collaboration is clearly more nuanced than we might have first thought. There are various types of collaboration and if you want to identify these various types, learning process analysis can assist you to do that, enabling you to identify the various types of collaboration with accuracy and reliability.

> You might want to allocate learners based on their approaches to collaboration, either for the benefit of the group or for the benefit of the learner—so they may acquire a broader set of approaches to collaboration. You may want to develop individuals with a more rounded approach to collaboration or develop in some learners' skills they do not currently have (and therefore use).

Collaboration for self-regulated learning

Another form of collaboration revealed by learning process analysis is where a learner collaborates primarily to facilitate their learning but with an eye to the group as well. In the example below (Figure 7.9) there are a few things happening. From an observable viewpoint this learner is asking one of their colleagues a question. The student's reasoning is on several fronts. First, they think it is important to check the clinical reasoning in this case, which is a significant component of this type of group work (problem-based learning in medicine). Second, there is a shared sense of collaborating by asking a question that might help other members of the group. And finally, this learner was unsure about something (symptom and diagnosis), which seems to be the main reason why the learner asked the question—to help their own learning.

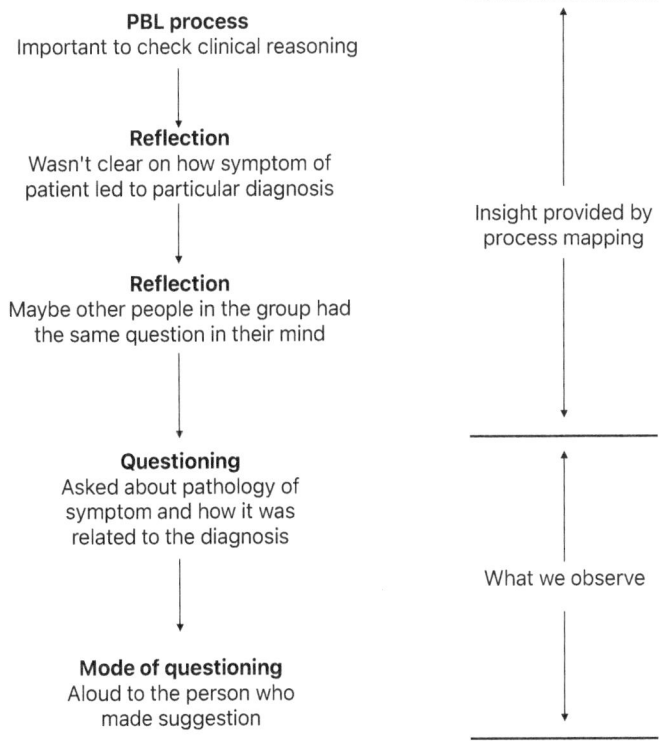

Figure 7.9: Learning process analysis revealing collaboration to facilitate learning for the individual and the group

As with all group work there may be some spin-off benefit for either the group, or other members of the group but the primary motivation for this decision was to address an understanding or knowledge gap. Another example of collaboration designed to facilitate the learner's knowledge by listening is below in figure 7.10. Again, this is an instance of what is rightfully regarded as collaboration.

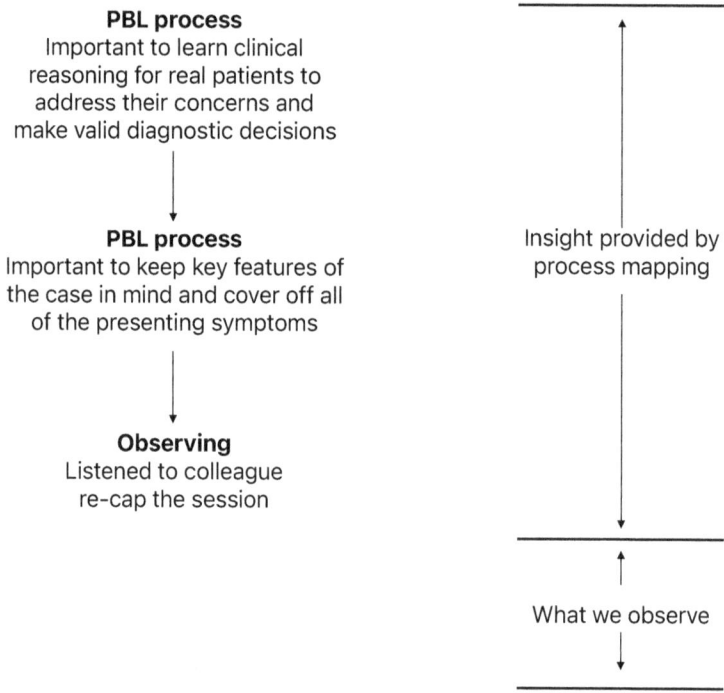

Figure 7.10: Learning process analysis revealing listening as part of learning

In summary, you can see that when we look at the decision-making of learners who collaborate, we find a range of decisions and a variety of reasons for why learners collaborate. Learners will collaborate purely for the benefit of the group and this form of collaboration can be as simple as staying silent and letting others speak. Alternatively, it can be a learner intervening in the dynamics of the group by engaging with a member or members of the group by bringing it back on track or making sure their contribution doesn't go too long so that others can contribute.

We have also seen that learners collaborate sometimes for their own benefit so that when they participate in the group, they do so primarily for their own benefit. It might be a gap in their learning or something they do not understand. Learners also collaborate for the group, not just in terms of group dynamics but also by offering information or answers to questions or asking a question to gain understanding.

Other soft skills, including critical thinking, teamwork (so closely allied with collaboration it might be seen as the same thing), problem solving and innovation are considerably more complex than we might think they are. They are not singular soft skills that once acquired can be moved about from one situation to the next. They are, just like collaboration, made up of a whole series of decision-making by learners that can be quite particular to learners from situation to situation. We have seen that we can gain access to the specific nature of these decisions through learning process analysis.

Mapping creativity and learning

Another soft skill, seen as important by industry and employers, is creativity. Creativity has been described by Forbes magazine as, 'the ability to imagine, dream and generate ideas'[22]. Creativity exists in many areas of schooling and insight into decision-making in art offers some insight into how learning process analysis may help learners get better at learning creativity. Understanding where learners got their ideas and why they decided to do their art in a particular way, with the particular materials they used are some insights into the creative process provided by learning process analysis. Creativity also exists at work and ideally in the form of innovation, whether that be new processes, structures, products or markets.

---

[22] Bernard Marr, The top 16 essential skills for the future of work. Forbes Magazine. September 12, 2022.

Learning process maps can be used to understand certain assessment items from the curriculum. For instance, to have 'students explain how ideas are represented in artworks', can be seen in several instances taken from the learning process map below (Figure 7.11) including the colours used and the background incorporated into this student's artwork.

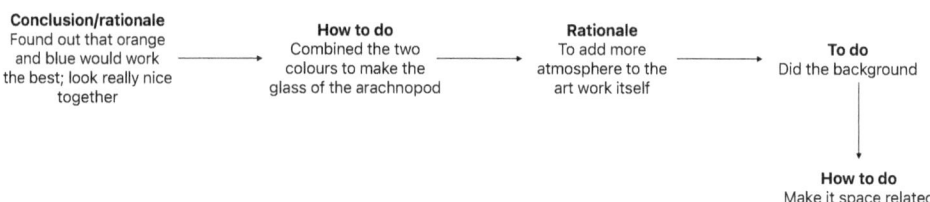

Figure 7.11: Part of a learning process map illustrating an avenue to assessment

Using learning process analysis in art can provide direction for future teaching and learning for a student or group of students. How they create effects and why they did so in a particular way are additional insights to be gained from learning process analysis (Figure 7.12).

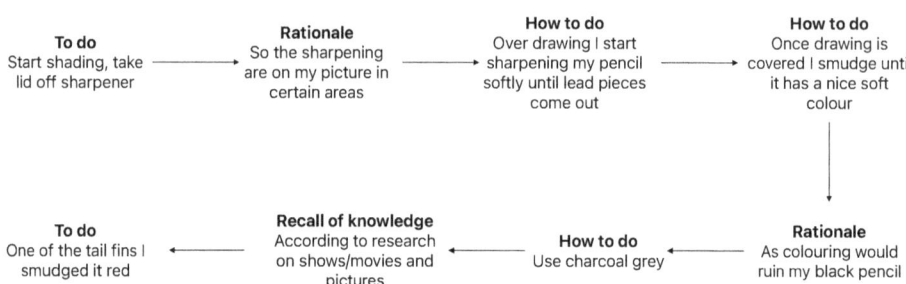

Figure 7.12: Learning process map showing a student's decision-making and reasons for creating effects in their artwork work

In line with the discussion above, we can also see how learners collaborate when they work on an art project.

Mapping critical thinking/clinical reasoning

Clinical reasoning skills are a specific outcome required by learners in a particular area—the clinical domain (nursing, physiotherapy, medicine etc). What distinguishes clinical reasoning is the amount of decision-making required to reach a firm and accurate diagnosis and the interrelationships between the decisions, data received and knowledge of the student. Learning process analysis reveals the intricate and often idiosyncratic nature of clinical reasoning.

Critical thinking—the ability to use trustworthy data to make decisions (Forbes, 2022, see footnote 22 above), is another of these soft skills that almost seems commonplace (that is, we all do it, or at least that is our perception) and might be viewed as an umbrella term that covers other sought-after skills such as clinical reasoning and the extension of critical thinking, complex decision-making.

Although clinical reasoning is really only part of this broader spectrum of soft skills it tends to attract more attention owing to its affiliation with the medical and allied health sector, which just about all of us interact with at some point. In many ways, clinical reasoning is similar to other soft skills like problem solving and communication skills in that it really is an amalgamation of many things including knowledge, experience and, of course, reasoning.

Part of what I am trying to achieve with my writing is to promote a better understanding of all these soft skills and other aspects of learning that are seen by many to be important for the workplace.

Take the example below (Figure 7.13), where medical students are engaged in a PBL exercise centred around a clinical presentation. As the student states, 'it is important to learn clinical reasoning ...' and it is this perception by the student that drives their behaviour in the PBL activity. What is notable is that without learning process analysis all of this thinking and decision-making remains unavailable.

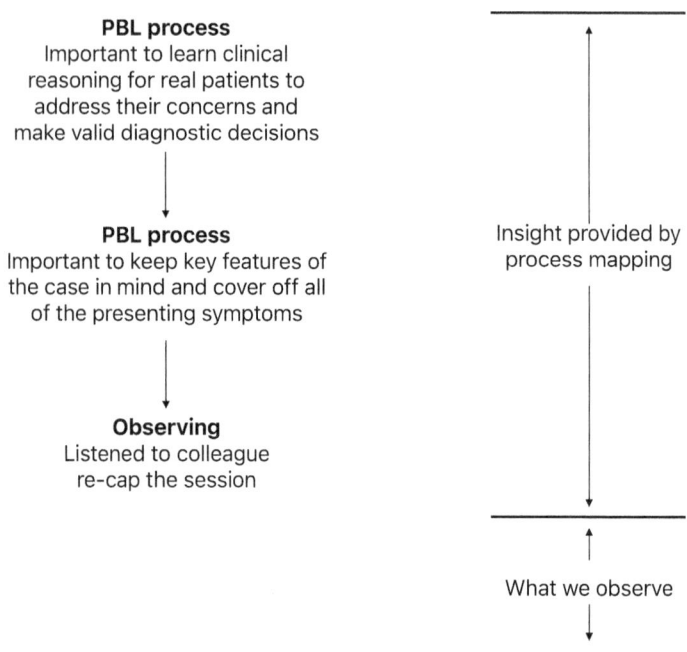

Figure 7.13: Learning process map showing nothing available to observe and all decision-making and reasoning via learning process analysis

By employing learning process analysis, we gain access to learners' reasoning while they are engaged in clinical reasoning. With that access we are able to understand the precise nature of clinical reasoning on an individual basis. We are able to understand why learners make the decisions they do and what decisions they make when beginning to use, acquire and practise clinical reasoning.

Small group work

Small group work, let's say anything between 2–10 students, is commonplace in education and learning. It is also common enough in the workplace, though it might be called a meeting in that context. Group work not only provides opportunities for learners to use a broad range of the soft skills described above, it also requires these skills to be used if the group is to be both effective and efficient. The sort of skills typically used in group work include collaboration, creativity, interpersonal communication, ethical behaviour, problem-solving, reasoning, self-directed learning, self-regulation and social and cultural awareness. I have shown with collaboration and clinical reasoning that all of these soft skills can be broken down into sets of decisions which are person-dependent. Collaboration, for example, can take multiple forms including identifying a discussion point, discussing ideas, comparing perspectives, contributing knowledge, questioning, exploring the meaning of something via the internet and reporting that back to the group and silence. To truly help learners get better at learning, we need to provide constructive feedback to them about how they approach group work.

Group work is very much a social process and tends to be more observable than a learner attempting a solitary task. Learning process analysis enables us to examine in detail learners' decision-making about what soft skills they used, how they used them and why they chose to do so, revealing what is below the observable surface.

Group work is also one of those aspects, specifically in education and in the workplace, where we struggle to determine the effectiveness of group members. In education we might ask group members to rate both theirs and others' contributions to the group as a form of a gatekeeping exercise and to ensure some sort of parity. So how do we know:

1. If someone is a productive group member?
2. How someone is being a productive group member?
3. Why are they contributing in these ways?

At work we want to know that people are contributing to the group whether it is a specific project or a regular meeting. In the boardroom it is important to establish that all directors are contributing and performing their roles as directors—an audit, if you like of directors' contributions. Of course, no matter the context, even the act of assessing these aspects of group dynamics and use of soft skills tends to focus the minds of those who are part of the group.

Using learning process analysis, we can provide evidence and feedback to workers, directors and their interested parties, learners and their teachers about how learners make decisions about collaborating and other soft skills as part of their contribution to a group.

So how can we do this in practice? Using one learner as an example I will show you that you can:

- detect which soft skills a student is using;
- how they are doing so;
- why they are doing so;
- determine the degree to which that student is a constructive member of a group; and
- provide feedback initially to the student and also how lessons can be learned for the group and future group work.

These examples, and the discussion around each example, will illustrate the utility of learning process analysis as a tool that can inform our understanding of group dynamics and how people contribute to groups so that we can use the lessons learned to produce more effective and efficient group work.

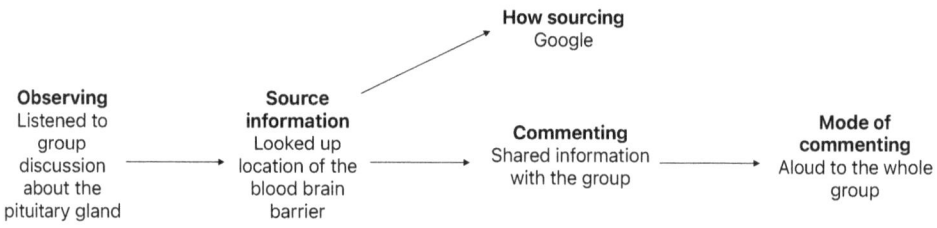

Figure 7.14

In the example above (Figure 7.14) what we observe is the group member listening, using their device to source data (Google) and then sharing information with the group. Of course, we expect to see this sort of decision-making in small groups so this decision is not particularly surprising. If we are to effectively understand how learners collaborate as an example of a soft skill and how that collaboration contributes to group dynamics, we need a tool such as learning process analysis to deliver clear data about who is doing what and why.

This latter element, the why, provides crucial insight into learning and enables us to assist learners to develop group collaboration skills and to be able to analyse each learner's contribution. In the next learning process map (Figure 7.15) we see a learner who is listening, is curious, willing to learn and conscious of group dynamics and wanting the group to work.

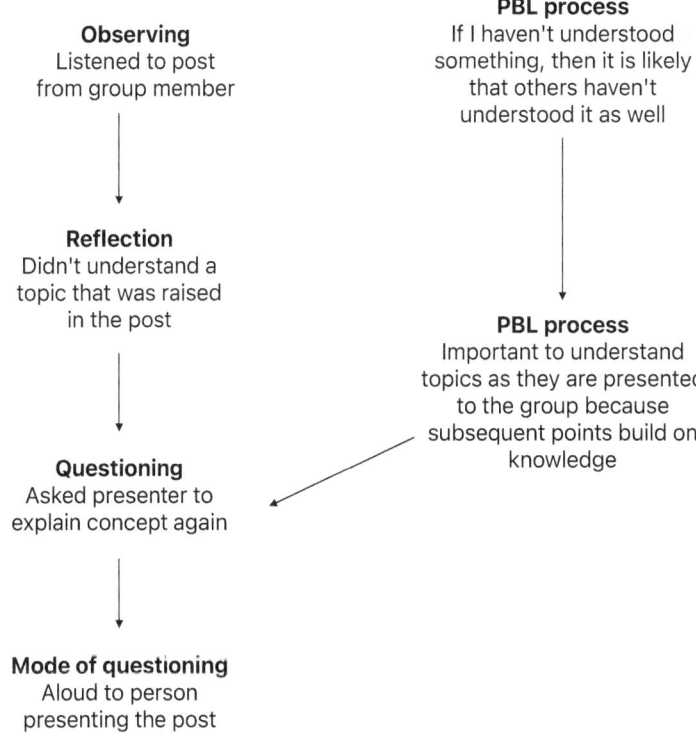

Figure 7.15 (2A1)

We also see the same learner (Figure 7.16) engaged in learning even though on the surface it would seem they are not obviously contributing to the group, other than by being quiet. This learner is self-directing their learning, listening to others in the hope it will benefit their own learning—a very clear and conscious decision about learning. In (Figure 7.17) there are multiple instances of this learner directing their learning ('PBL's can support other clinical skills …', 'important to be thorough …') and in (Figure 7.18) exhibiting that awareness of group dynamics ('Important to be patient to maintain group dynamics' and 'listened to what others have to say first …').

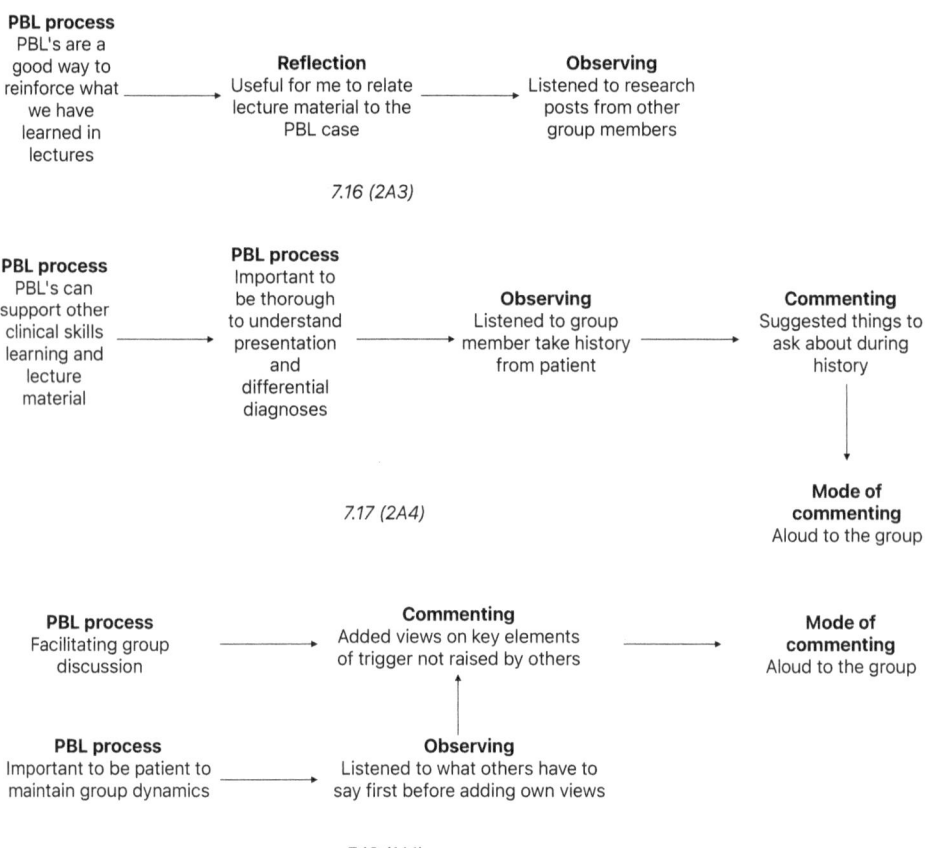

Figures 7.16, 7.17 and 7.18

How can this play out in the practicalities of the classroom? A typical report on a student will use language like, 'demonstrating outstanding achievement of …' or 'demonstrating limited achievement of …' an agreed standard[23]. I think it is generally agreed that there is a degree of fog associated with reports such as these. They do not include a deep dive into what a learner can do other than for measured assessments of content or quality of product (such as art). In terms of how a learner learns these reports are at best opaque. Using learning process analysis, we can say with clear evidence that the learner above is a self-regulating learner who is curious, willing to learn and conscious of group dynamics. This approach to measuring how people learn can be used across a broad spectrum of subjects and activities and can also be applied beyond the classroom, particularly in the case of group work.

Using learning process analysis, we can also see where ideas are discussed and gain insight into how those ideas are generated. In the two examples below from another learner we can determine that, in the first instance (Figure 7.19) they have had a thought about the topic at hand, which is based on their previous knowledge and they share their thinking with the group. This is the sort of decision-making we want to see during group work. We want students to hypothesise and think about what is in front of them, and with learning process analysis we can detect which students are doing this and those who are not. We can use this

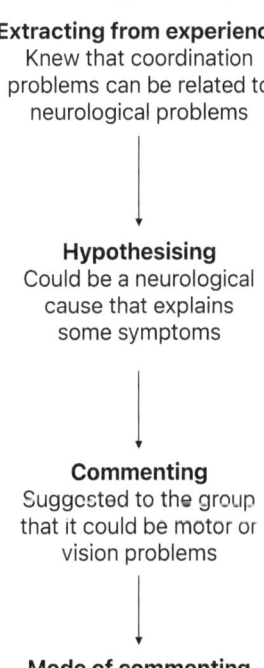

Figure 7.19

---

[23] See for example, https://www.education.act.gov.au/public-school-life/assessment_and_reporting/act-student-reporting accessed 7 July 2024.

information to assist those learners who might not engage in this approach to learning.

By seeing the intricacies of why learners do what they do when learning in groups we can gain insight into details that previously we could only guess at. For example, a learner being actively interested in course content so they can direct their learning, something we want from our learners, is revealed by the learning process map below (Figure 7.20).

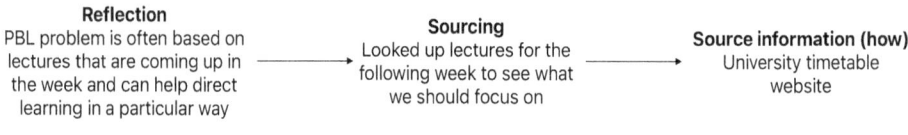

Figure 7.20

Knowing that some learners are actively engaged in these ways and having clear data that reveals who is not so engaged is the sort of feedback that enables us to work with learners who would benefit from input into how they could improve how they learn.

Social constructivism

Social constructivism is a process where learning can occur when a learner recognises that they do not know something and this recognition prompts them to seek meaning or understanding and they do so with other learners. The following two examples (Figure 7.21) show this aspect of social constructivism in action, one decision is to look something up and the other is to ask a question to the group.

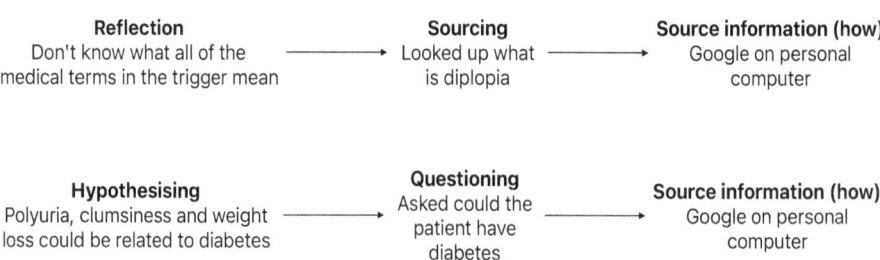

Figure 7.21: Social constructivism in action

The practical use

Learners adopt a diverse range of approaches to learning. Aided by increased visibility from learning process analysis, greater insight into what learners do when they are learning can only help us to help them, particularly given these unique approaches learners adopt when learning.

The primary function of learning process analysis is to display learners' conscious decisions and the reasons for those decisions, sequentially. Each learning process map represents a learner's decision-making. Learning process analysis also provides a means of illustrating how learners' decisions relate to each other. Learning process analysis enables us to compare the decisions learners make about processes, from one learning event to the next.

Feedback is critical for learning. Learning process analysis's greatest asset is that it can interrogate learning at the individual level and provide detailed feedback about how learners go about using specific processes such as: rationalising or reflecting as above; or hypothesising and questioning as other examples. Learning process analysis can detect the use of these skills in any learner, in any context, from one content area to another and can provide clear feedback to both the learner and teacher about how effectively learners are employing their skills and why they are doing so. With feedback of this nature at their disposal, learners and teachers can work on improving the use of these skills no matter what the task, from one classroom to another or from one context to another. We also gain insight into the motivation of learners—why they choose to ask questions or why they choose a particular strategy.

That is, learning process analysis can provide accurate feedback to both learners and teachers about how learners learn. This method of understanding learning is not about transferring skills across contexts. Rather, it is that these skills are used in different contexts (which we know) and that this process can detect and show how these skills are used no matter the context and, more importantly, no matter who is using them.

These conscious decisions of learners, once revealed, can provide evidence that furthers our understanding about such things as how learners construct knowledge, their level of skill acquisition and their attitudes and values. These decisions provide data about the nature of learning for each and every learner; data that digs down deeper, beyond the surface layer of learning exhibited in the classroom, or anywhere else for that matter and which shows the variability in any classroom in a readily examinable way and on an individual basis which can benefit both teachers and learners.

It is this variability in learners' approaches to learning that contributes to the difficulty of matching the learning environment (including teaching, tasks and assessment) to the needs, or indeed wants, of a learner and which ultimately determines the learning that occurs. If we are to fully assist learners to gain the most from their learning experiences, we require insight into learning in an individualised form. Detecting variability in skill use, making sense of it and providing this information to both learners and teachers in a form that makes sense to them, can result in consistently greater achievement of learning intentions. That is, more learners achieving more, more often.

As people try to learn, they will make decisions about many things. To collaborate, to share a resource, to ask a question, to take notes, to stop working and to have a break, to engage in the task, to listen to a colleague, to listen instead of asking a question, to seek feedback. These decisions that learners make cover all aspects of learning, in any learning environment at any age of learning. Whether the learner is successful, or unsuccessful, is engaged or disengaged, or is online, in-person or something else, they are making decisions about learning and about the process of learning. These decisions may be quite minute and concentrated on one area, like how to subtract or divide or multiply using times tables for a younger learner. For an older school-aged learner it might be how they use their free time.

The name of the game in educational contexts is learning. All educators at all levels of learning have an expectation that their students will learn something. That is pretty much the starting point in the professional engagement of teachers with learners. The often requested and mentioned next step is for learners to be more knowledgeable about how to learn and for them to be able to self-regulate and/or self-direct their learning. If we want learners to be able to develop their ability to be self-regulating/directing learners, they need to have insight into how they approach their learning. Learning process analysis can show in forensic detail how each learner goes about their learning.

Learning process analysis can provide data that shows that various learners work best and learn best in similar ways. There may be groupings of how learners approach their learning and learning process analysis can show that. Most importantly this information can be fed back to learners so they are clearer about how they learn best and what works best for them and they can use this information about their learning to start developing more finely tuned and effective approaches to learning and be more informed about their learning and be in a better position to get better at learning.

Learning process analysis is highly practical and has the potential to provide insight to teachers about which learners need greater input from them and which learners can be left to work more independently knowing they have the skills and the decision-making toolkit that enables them to be effective learners.

Learning about problem solving

So, what is the practical use? Take problem-solving for example. We are told that there is no such generic skill as problem solving. Yet, we are reminded on a fairly regular basis that school prepares the workers of the future and indeed so does any educational institution. We are also reminded that employers want people who can problem solve and who have soft skills such as communication skills, collaboration and teamwork skills and are critical thinkers.

Clearly problem solving is a cognitive process. It may be that everyone solves problems entirely uniquely and idiosyncratically. How a student solves a problem or problems can be mapped and used as the basis for feedback to that student on an individual basis. They can then use that feedback, as one would for any feedback about any skill, to improve their ability to carry out that skill, or to problem solve in this case.

The results of problem solving can be readily determined. Is the problem solved or not and to what extent? Learning process analysis can provide a map of the decision-making processes about problem solving that the student employed and this information can serve as the focus for both the student and the teacher to improve problem solving skills. If they are particularly successful in some areas but not in others, we can detect that and this can be shared and form the basis of a strategy for improvement.

If learners are to develop multiple strategies of learning it will be helpful if there is a tool which can provide feedback to learners about which strategies they are using and why they chose to use them at any given point in time. John Hattie reminds us 'there is no one way of learning' and I agree wholeheartedly with that statement. Equally he states that there is no one 'set of understandings that unravel the processes of learning'[24]. Learning process analysis is, however, an avenue to understanding the ways learners learn and the various processes of learning utilised by learners. Using learning process analysis frees up learners to engage in a range of strategies for learning, safe in the knowledge that these approaches work and that they can keep on getting better at learning.

---

[24] Hattie, J. Visible Learning for Teachers. Routledge. 2011 (p. 103) see https://www.taylorfrancis.com/chapters/mono/10.4324/9780203181522-13/flow-lesson-learning-john-hattie

CHAPTER EIGHT

How to use learning process maps to help learners

Introduction

Having established that you want to use learning process analysis and why you want to do so, the next step is to understand how to go about using learning process maps to assist you with that purpose.

This chapter is a step-by-step guide for 'how to use learning process maps' to help your learners get better at learning. How to collect the data you need to construct learning process maps—including using stimulated recall interviewing with your students to drill down into their reasoning. Once you have all this information your next step is to construct the learning process maps, including classifying (coding, categorising) the elements of the learning process map (decisions and reasons) and the structure of the learning process map (which element connects to which element). How these steps can be done is described and explained using worked examples throughout the rest of this chapter. I will be revisiting quite a few of the concepts you have already met, such as assigning categories to decisions and what learning process analysis can reveal. All of this revisiting is intended to reinforce the method that is required to use learning process analysis successfully—for that is what learning process analysis is—a method.

Having completed your maps, you will want to start exploring the detail of the maps—analysing and making sense of them. Your approach will depend on your original purpose. You might be interested in examining the maps of just one learner. You might want to compare a learner's maps over time or take a snapshot of their learning at a particular point in time. You might wish to compare maps between two or more learners.

Equally, you might be exploring achievement of outcomes and how the learning process maps might inform your understanding of why and how a learner is achieving outcomes, or not achieving outcomes. And you might want to complete that same exercise for two or more learners, again, determined by your original purpose. To reiterate, the driver for interrogating your students' maps will be why you wanted to use learning process analysis in the first place.

There are other matters to consider before you embark on your learning process analysis journey. Depending on the policies governing research in your workplace, if you are conducting research, you may have to formally obtain either ethics approval and/or permission from those who can legally give it, to conduct the interviews. That said, the overall aim of this book is to encourage teachers to use learning process analysis as part of their formative feedback toolkit to help learners get better at learning. Given that aim, for most teachers, permission is not required as it will be part of normal learning and teaching interactions that take place in your classroom. Much the same goes for using it in the workplace—a means to helping people at work get better outcomes.

Using video to capture decision-making

I want to share with you how to collect the necessary data to construct your learning process maps using video to capture learners' decision-making. Context is important when trying to assist learners and it is no different when using videoing to start your data collection. There are a few key considerations to take into account.

The duration of the activity or task you are videoing is an important consideration. Using video as your initial data collection phase will produce a large volume of data. The volume depends on how many students you are videoing and for how long. Remembering that you also need to follow up with interviewing each individual learner to extract all their decision-making and their reasons. It may be that the realities of the classroom, or the workplace for that matter, will restrict your use of video as an initial data collection.

The nature of the environment needs to be considered. If you are videoing learners, aside from required permissions, the environment needs to be suitable for videoing of learners, preferably an open setting and a clear line of sight for the cameras. If your purpose is to explore how students in a small group setting work together then videoing will be ideally suited to that purpose. Finally, various systems will have policies, procedures and/or guidelines regarding the videoing of young and/or vulnerable people and you need to be both aware of and act in accordance with, these requirements.

The tasks you put to your learners should be sufficiently open-ended to encourage the making of a range of decisions by learners. If you were teaching science, the task set for the students might be along the lines of: 'design an investigation to find out as much as you can about the ways that plants and animals interact with each other'. And if you were teaching art the task might be along the lines of: 'choosing your topic, materials and methods, produce an artwork to be considered for the school art show.'

You will want to strategically edit the video to about twenty minutes of running time. That will result in about a forty-minute interview, which is a significant chunk of time in any learner's, or teacher's, day. Be clear about your rationale for your editing, ensuring you focus on the key elements of the task that are relevant to the learner. Getting used to editing will take a little practice, so you might want to start using smaller chunks of time. In essence, what might look like a learner doing little may well be a learner making a whole series of decisions. For this reason, edit your video as deliberately as possible in order to ensure that each learner was undertaking a range of activities. As I said, this will take time to get right.

The video recording provides a means of illustrating to the learner what they were doing and is used as a prompt for what are called, 'stimulated recall interviews' (SRI). SRI uses video data as a prompt to guide questions regarding the decisions learners make during the task and has been successfully employed for many years to gather accurate data in a range of health education and education settings.

When interviewing, your questions need to be as open as they can be without losing focus on the learning you are interested in. You want to know whether the learner has made a conscious decision and what that decision was.

With the video paused on the particular frame you are interested in, ask questions along the lines of the following:

1. Did you make a conscious decision there?
2. What was that decision?
3. Why did you make that decision?
4. Did you make any other decisions about this? (and, if required)
5. What were those decisions?
6. Why did you make that (or those) decision/s?

(Repeat questions 4 through 6 as required.)

> Useful tip[25]
>
> Occasionally, a learner may reply, 'I don't know' in response to a question. One useful follow-up to this response is to ask, 'what would it be if you did know?' This follow-up question has generally elicited an answer that was there all along.

---

[25] This tip comes straight out of Susan Scott's book, Fierce Conversations 1999. Penguin. New York.

Finally, you will want to audio record the interview so that you have the information on hand when drawing up your learning process maps.

The initial function of learning process analysis is that it visibly represents learners' decisions sequentially. Each learning process map represents a learner's decisions about processes (like investigating, looking something up, hypothesising) for a single interview prompt. You might think each learner will, or should, have the same number of prompts. However, the nature of learning is not an even distribution of decision-making or contributions and so some learners may have many and others very few, for the same task.

A learning process map is constructed from the learners' answers and not from supposition on your part. Two examples illustrate this principle of learning process map construction (Figures 8.1 and 8.2).

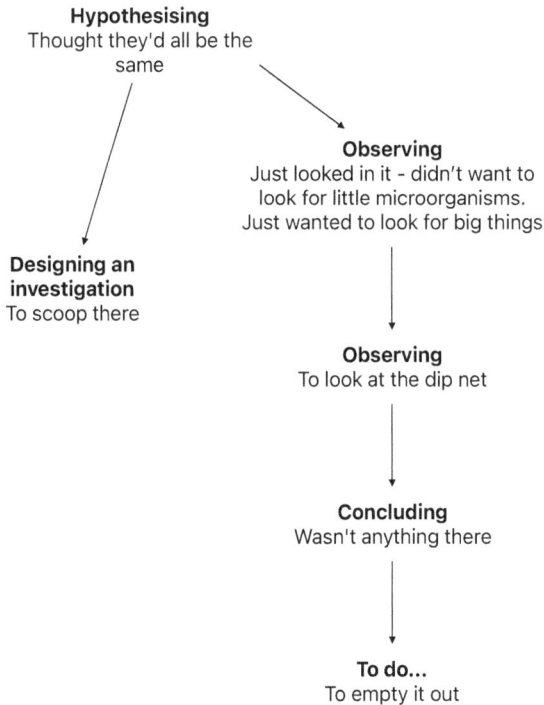

Figure 8.1: Learning process map of a learner in junior science

This first example (Figure 8.1) is from a junior high school learner undertaking an open-ended investigation in science. The reason given for the decision about 'how to observe' was that the learner 'just wanted to look for big things'. So, what we have is a learner deciding to hypothesise and because of this they made a series of other decisions. The learner was not asked whether the original decision was about hypothesising but whether or not they made a decision and what that decision was. The type of process and the nature of the decision was a matter of categorisation and was completed after the interview.

A different example from a different area of learning, medical education, also illustrates this principle (Figure 8.2).

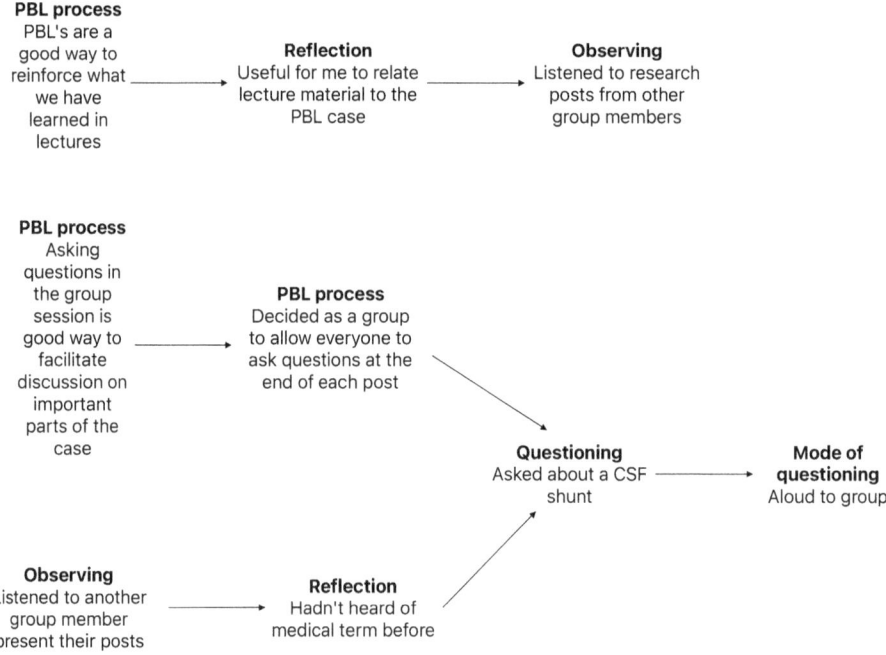

Figure 8.2: Learning process map from a student in a PBL tutorial

This example is of a learner, a first-year medical student, engaging in group work who made a decision to 'ask about a CSF [cerebral spinal fluid] shunt.' The reasons they did this were multiple: 'because asking questions is a good way to facilitate' and 'because the group decided ...' as well as because they 'hadn't heard of medical term before', which came about because they 'were listening ...'. This example is more complex with multiple decisions and multiple reasons.

It is important to take the time to translate the interview data into learning process maps, making sure to determine whether what you have in front of you is a decision, a reason or a reason for making a decision that is also a decision. This step is the same for data collected by video, proforma or other means.

The next example shows the interview data, the process of categorisation and the resultant learning process map.

Interviewer: Did you make a conscious decision there? (and if yes, then) What was that decision?

Shane: 'Yes, to dip the net.'

[There was no response to 'Why did you make that decision?']

Interviewer: Did you make any other decisions about this? What were those decisions?

Shane: 'To dip the net from the edge of the boardwalk.'

Interviewer: Why did you make that (or those) decision/s?

Shane: 'Just went there.'

Interviewer: Did you make any other decisions about this? What were those decisions?

Shane: 'To use the dip net.'

Interviewer: Why did you make that (or those) decision/s?

Shane: 'Easier.'

The student's responses were translated into learning process maps by first categorising their decisions. This required a determination of which process the decision was about and whether it was one of three types of decision. Those types were:

- to use that process (what process to use); or
- how to go about that process (how to use a process); or
- where to use that process (where to use a process).

Once the responses were categorised, they were placed in the order in which they were given by the learner. In some cases, reasons given by learners were categorised as also being decisions. This student's responses were categorised and ordered as indicated in Figure 8.3. For example, the decision 'to dip net' was categorised as a decision 'to design an investigation'.

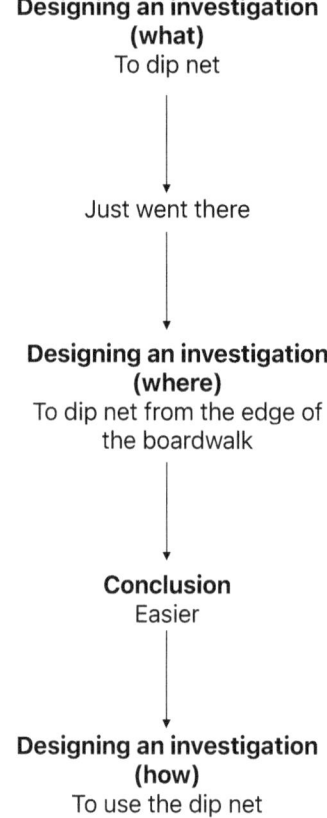

Figure 8.3: Learning process map with categories

Using proforma data capture

In many ways using a proforma[26] to capture learners' decisions has advantages over using video. For most learning tasks you can

---

[26] A proforma in this context is a blank form with areas for learners to write down their decisions. Examples are provided at the end of this chapter.

target the proforma towards a particular section of that task or learning episode. Take a science investigation, for instance. You could target the:

- designing of the investigation;
- choice of research question or questions;
- conducting of their investigation;
- design of the method used by the learner;
- nature of collaboration between learners in a group investigation; and
- nature of their results presentation or their conclusion and why they came to that conclusion (on what was their conclusion based?).

Design the proforma to suit your or your students' areas of interest, which may vary from student to student and from class to class.

Another advantage of a proforma is that it hands control over to the learner so that they can write down their decisions when, for instance, designing a research question for an investigation in science. If you were videoing the same investigation, it would be difficult to tell when these decisions were being made just by looking at the video. By targeting a specific aspect of a learning activity, you can gather a lot of data about a learner's decision-making about a specific component of the curriculum. So what you get from a proforma is clarity of purpose, better use of time and resources (efficiency) and feedback designed to promote learning.

Learners will generally be able to write down quite readily what decisions they make over certain timeframes. By confining that timeframe to a shorter or specific element of a task you can capture a lot of detail about specific components. You can also target different components for different learners, and there is no requirement for you to target the same element for all learners at the same time. The overall result is flexibility and efficiency and feedback that is more likely to help the learner get better at learning.

Adapting the proforma to the activity is the best approach to adopt. If you want to capture as many decisions as possible and you are able to do that without interfering with the business of learning then you should use that approach. A colleague and I used this approach when we were looking at the decision-making of medical students engaged in PBL. We adapted the proforma to mimic the stages of PBL so that the students could write down any decisions they made at the very beginning of the first session and at various stages through to the end of the problem. PBL, at least in medical schools, generally consists of a small group (up to about nine students) learning structure that requires students to make sense of a patient presentation (i.e. the patient is presenting herself to the doctor with particular symptoms).

The structure of the PBL follows identifying the cues, formulating the problem, brainstorming (what could be happening here?), generating and organising tentative hypotheses (causes and mechanisms of what they think might be the cause of the presentation), identifying learning issues for individual study and reporting back. PBL, by design, places students into areas where they are meeting concepts and processes which they need to understand to make sense of the patient's presentation—part of the deal is they will go and research these 'learning issues' and present back to their colleagues. Multiple iterations of these steps, or at least part of these steps, occur with the learners arriving at what they think is their diagnosis and, based on their diagnosis, students determine what management they think is appropriate for the person.

It is a complex, group-based learning structure with many opportunities for learners to make decisions about what they do and why. Structurally there might be two or three sessions of 1 hour to 1 and 1/2 hours with a PBL tutor to assist the students and keep them on track. Students in PBL have been shown to make many decisions about how they learn, what they learn and why they do what they do. It tends to be a dynamic and engaging learning environment and is exactly the sort of environment that suits using a proforma. We adapted the proforma along the lines of the stages the students went through and left it up to the students to write down any decisions they made throughout the course of the PBL. In this context the PBL was three sessions of 90 minutes duration and spread out over the course of seven days (to enable students to research their learning issues and prepare presentations for their colleagues).

The key to any proforma is that it needs to match up closely to the activity, or part-activity in which you are interested. Finally, the important follow-up to the proforma is the interview based on what is written in the proforma. In the next section I will describe the nature of interviewing based on either video data or proforma data.

Stimulated Recall Interviewing

At this stage you will have either a collection of completed proformas or a collation of edited and/or annotated video data. One of these items will be your starting point for the next step in learning process analysis—which is interviewing your learners using either the video or proforma as the basis for what is known as a SRI. Stimulated recall interviews are used in many fields, including educational research, and without the interview much of the very useful data we ultimately extract from learning process maps would be unavailable.

Your interview goal is to try and gain a clear understanding of what decisions your learners made about the task in which they were engaged and why they made these decisions. It is vitally important to establish the learner:

- made a conscious decision;
- states or re-confirms what that decision was;
- describes why they made that decision;
- describes, if relevant, how they made that decision and if possible, why;
- describes, if relevant, when they made that decision and if possible, why;

- describes, if relevant, where they made that decision and if possible, why; and
- made any other decisions that pre-empted and led to the decision evident in the video or described in the proforma (many of which will be covered by the above three enquiries).

By drilling down beyond the decision written down or observed and establishing *why, how, when* and or *where* learners made a decision, you are likely to uncover additional decisions, with reasons, that complete the decision-making sequence that accurately describes and provides insight into how they were approaching their learning at a particular point in time. Ideally, the more open your questioning is, the better, albeit focused on the making of their decisions about learning. Be prepared to wait for a response and don't suggest answers. The risk with suggesting an answer is that it may be your thinking that is displayed in the learning process map, not the learner's. Start by establishing whether the learner made a conscious decision and the nature of that decision. The words used for this initial question will vary a little depending on whether the prompt for the interview is a video or a proforma.

Typically, your interview questions will be similar to those described below.

a) (For video) Did you make a conscious decision there? Note: It may be necessary to play the video back and forth to help the learner's recollection.
b) (For proforma) Is that a conscious decision? (Or words to that effect, referring to the written decision on the proforma.)
c) What was that decision? Describe it for me. (It will not hurt for a student using a proforma to reiterate what is already written down.)
d) Why did you make that decision? Or, if this question doesn't elicit a response, 'what was your reason for making

that decision'? Or an alternative to this type of question, without any suggestion of an answer. And don't forget Susan Scott's advice[27] if you need help.

There are additional questions to ask depending on the nature of the learning process analysis exercise. These questions are described below.

e) Did you make any other decisions about this?
f) What were those decisions? It is useful here to also explore any reasons for those decisions.

Another useful set of follow-up questions, especially to a learner's description of their reason for a decision is to ask: why was that? Or, why is that the case?

The following example illustrates how the interview, including the responses, translates into a learning process map. This example is taken from a junior science class (learners aged 15 years old) conducting an investigation at a local field study centre. The example will include:

1. a typical interview script;
2. the resulting learning process map; and
3. a refresher about how to read and start to make sense of a learning process map.

The interview script (the learner's pseudonym is Shane)

Interviewer: Did you make a conscious decision there? (and if yes, then) What was that decision?

Shane: Yes, to dip net.

[There was no response to Why did you make that decision?]

Interviewer: Did you make any other decisions about this? What were those decisions?

---

[27] To remind you: Susan's tip is: *If a learner should respond to any question with "I don't know" a very useful follow-up question is to ask: 'What would it be if you did know?'*

Shane:	To dip net from the edge of the boardwalk.
Interviewer:	Why did you make that (or those) decision/s?
Shane:	Just went there.
Interviewer:	Did you make any other decisions about this? What were those decisions?
Shane:	To use the dip net.
Interviewer:	Why did you make that (or those) decision/s?
Shane:	Easier.

The resulting learning process map

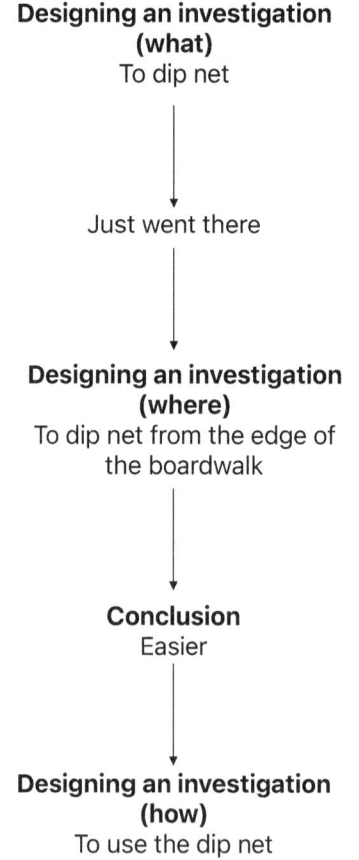

Figure 8.4: Shane's learning process map

At this stage it is worthwhile to practise going from a proforma to interview to learning process map. Keep the focus fairly general in nature, not critical to the student's learning and short in time, maybe 5–10 minutes at best. It may be something as simple as, 'design an investigation to explore … (insert relevant topic)' or any other accessible and open task for the learner. The key practice point here is to be able to step back and let the learner make the decisions about how they approach the task, or even, if confidence permits, what task they wish to undertake.

Some practice exercises—constructing learning process maps

To assist you with that practice a couple of exercises follow. These exercises provide the script of the interview so that your task will be to convert the text from a stimulated recall interview into a learning process map. One example is based on proforma data and the other is based on video data. Pencil and paper might be easiest at first, though by all means use your favourite software, if you find that more comfortable. For your feedback the 'answer learning process map' for each script is provided at the end of this chapter.

Exercise 1 (based on video data—year 9 science learner)

Your task is to convert the following script into a learning process map.

Interviewer:	Did you make a conscious decision there? (And if yes) What was that decision?
Learner A:	Yes, to dip a net.
Interviewer:	Why did you make that decision?
Learner A:	Wanted to catch something.
Interviewer:	Did you make any other decisions about this? What were those decisions?
Learner A:	To dip a net at the north edge of the pond.

Interviewer:	Why did you make that decision?
Learner A:	Hadn't been there and wanted to see what was there. Someone found an eel there.

(Solution at Figure 8.13)

Exercise 2 (based on proforma data—medical student)

Your task is to convert the following script into a learning process map.

Interviewer:	Can we go to the next decision on the sheet? You have written down, 'asked a PBL team member about a previous post on the same symptom.' Was that your decision?
Learner H:	Yes.
Interviewer:	Why did you make that decision?
Learner H:	Remembered the same symptoms from a previous case but couldn't remember the details.
Interviewer:	Why was that?
Learner H:	Vomiting was a sign in the trigger.
Interviewer:	How did you go about asking that question?
Learner H:	Aloud, to one other student in the group.

(Solution at Figure 8.14)

    This probing of learners' decision-making via video/proforma --> stimulated recall interviewing --> construction of process-maps and analysis of these learning process maps is a form of microanalysis. The most useful description of microanalysis comes from Cleary and Sandars (2011)[28] who describe it as: 'a highly specific or fine-grained form of measurement that targets

---

[28] See Cleary, T. J., & Sandars, J. (2011). Assessing self-regulatory processes during clinical skill performance: a pilot study. *Med Teach, 33*(7), e368-374. doi:10.3109/0142159X.2011.577464

behaviours or processes as they occur in real time across authentic contexts', like classrooms.

In time and with practice, you will become more skilled at interviewing and drilling down into learners' decision-making and both you and your learners will benefit from that experience. The next section will take you through the step of categorising decisions and adding this information to your maps.

Constructing maps

The first step is to set your overall learning goals, purpose and then appropriate tasks you think will enable learners to achieve those goals.

You need to extract data from your students about their decision-making while they are undertaking a task. The nature of the task and the sort of data you are wanting to extract will dictate what approach you use to extract learners' decision-making about learning. The main sources of data will be either video or a proforma (see Figure 8.5).

Figure 8.5: Methods of constructing learning process maps

As described previously, video data will provide you with access to a broader range of decision-making and has the advantage of recording what happened. Video data enables you to replay sections where decision-making occurred. It is however, more logistically complex and will tend to reduce the number of learners on which you can focus your learning process analysis activities.

Using a proforma will enable you to reach more learners, though may capture less decision-making. A well-designed proforma is easier to use and with good interview technique, will capture a significant amount of data, from which you can develop your maps.

Until artificial intelligence or some other form of programming can reliably convert the video/proforma data + interview data into accurate learning process maps, constructing these maps is a manual task[29]. With this in mind, the basic steps to follow are:

- accurately transcribe your interview data;
- determine which data are decisions, which are reasons and how they connect with each other (the 'flow'). It is important to ensure that the final order accurately reflects the learner's thinking and decision-making;
- an additional step is to run your drafted maps by the learners so they can confirm the accuracy of the learning process map; and
- it is important to ensure these steps are completed in a timely manner.

Constructing a learning process map—from video data

I will walk you through an example, describing how we move from initial decision to reasons for those decisions (via proforma/video and interview) to the final constructed learning process map. This example comes from the sporting arena.

Digital edited video data is readily available and used by professional sports. In the case of the footballer, the action observed on an edited video was:

– Player 2 kicking the ball out in front of player 3 (so that player 3 could run on to it).

The first question asked, was to confirm the decision made, which was:

– 'to kick the ball out in front of player 3'.

As you have seen, we use learning process analysis to understand what decisions were made and why those decisions were made. Our next interview question was:

---

[29] Some colleagues and I are currently researching this very aspect – using AI to create learning process maps.

- why did you make that decision?
- the answer being 'because player 3 has speed'.

Sport is made up of many of these decisions by each and every player and so we want to gain as much understanding about why player 2 came to that decision for that reason and so we can use the interview to probe deeper:

- how did that come about (seeing player 3)?

With the answer being:

- I looked into the centre of the ground.

So, what we have done is start from the observed action (particularly in sport where assuming why actions occur is risky and unhelpful and not conducive to ongoing improvement—i.e. getting better) and worked backwards from there. Effectively, we have reverse-engineered the 'making of the decision'.

To construct the learning process map we want to end up with the final decision as the end point of the map. The questioning sequence in the interview starts at that point (the observed decision made) and works backward from there (having exhausted all possible reasons why a decision was made). The learning process map presents the information in a time-forward manner starting with the final reason given ('looked in the centre of the ground'), any decision/observation that followed this reason (saw player 3), then the next reason ('player 3 has speed')—and this particular player really does have speed to burn—and finally the decision made (to kick the ball in front of player 3). That is, it represents the sequence as it happened both internally (from learning process analysis) and externally (observed and confirmed by learning process analysis).

The following diagram illustrates this sequence of interviewing and the answers provided, which form the basis of a learning process map.

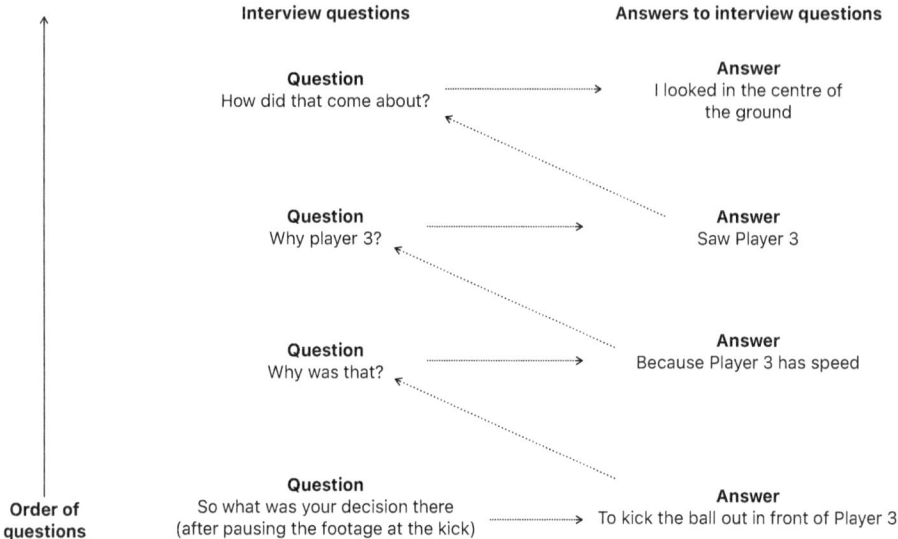

Figure 8.6: Learning process map interview sequence

The resultant learning process map shows the time-sequenced decision-making:

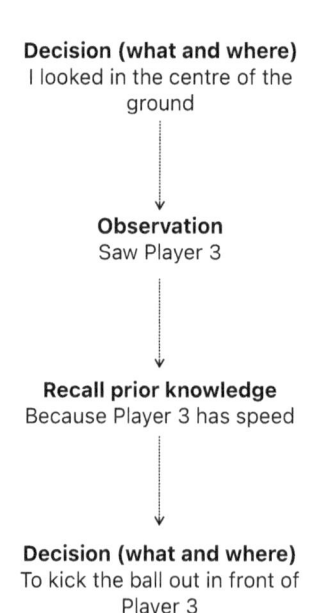

Figure 8.7: Learning process map from the above interview transcript

Constructing a learning process map—from proforma data

The following learning process map comes from an interview after a student had completed a proforma. The interview format is a little different to a SRI based on video data, mainly because some of the decision-making of the student has already been made available, via the proforma.

The proforma is provided below. Student L

Part of PBL session	Things I did	(Space for student responses)
Making sense of and discussing the trigger	Asked questions?	
	Looked something up?	
	Listened to colleagues?	Yes
Explanations for clinical presentation	Asked questions?	

Figure 8.8: Part of a proforma from PBL student

Section of interview transcript (edited for ease of reading):

Session 1

Student L: 'So, in session one, I suggest that some key phrases in the trigger and discuss what's reasonable for some symptoms as in the vomiting, you know, not ignoring.'

Interviewer: So why, why that?

Student L: 'Well, I think that due to being asked about particular symptoms, is this a reasonable symptom to have and we sort of were working out or with the vomiting and a young boy … this is hard food poisoning or something, it's not an almost symptom. So, what's reasonable was related to what **the tutor sort of asked about with the symptoms.** And then obviously he ... was like, what are the key things within this, which most of the time is the trigger anyway ... **I just volunteered to say stuff because sometimes not anyone else does, so someone's got to say stuff.**'

Interviewer: How so?

Student L: **'Just to the group'**

Figure 8.9 shows the learning process map for this transcript. The main elements of the learning process map are taken from the responses in bold above.

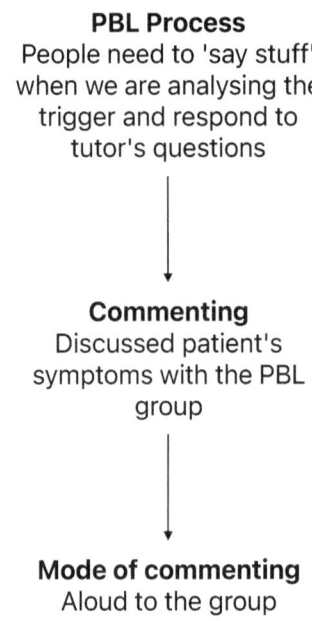

Figure 8.9: The resultant learning process map derived from the proforma and interview data

Assigning categories of decisions and reasons

Categories are an important basis for analysing and comparing learning process maps. Investing time into getting this component of learning process analysis as right as you can, will pay dividends when it comes to helping leaners to get better at learning.

The range of decision categories is large and may well vary from one area of learning (science, art or medicine) or activity (business, sport) to another. You will need to decide for yourself which are the most appropriate categories to use for your particular area of learning or activity. To help you with that I have provided examples below of the text from interviews, the learning process maps produced from this interview data and the categories applied to each decision/reason. It is not all bad news. There is some commonality across learning in the processes used but just as each specific area of learning tends to have its own language, the same applies to the categories in learning process analysis.

The most basic of categorised decisions made by learners embrace those processes and skills described throughout this book. The more familiar of these skills include observing, collaborating, hypothesising, inferring, deducing, reflecting, concluding, investigating and designing an investigation. We also see very clear evidence of learners engaging in self-directed learning, self-regulating learning and engaging in various categories of critical thinking, including clinical reasoning.

Although having a comprehensive list of all possible decision-making might be nice 'to have', the reality is that with the idiosyncratic nature of learning although we will capture most categories of decision-making, such a list will be one that develops and expands as we continue to develop our understanding of how people learn.

Currently we can describe a broad range of categories of decision-making in learning. Beginning with more general and better-known categories we can show that learners make the following decisions. Most of these descriptions are of commonly understood actions by learners: observing, investigating, asking questions and so forth. What the descriptions below capture are learners' decision-making about these components of learning.

Decision categories:

There are some categories of decision-making that are generic in that they are used across different contexts and no matter what the context, the definition/description of these categories remains unchanged. And then there are categories of decision-making that will be particular to specific contexts, such as science investigations, art projects, exercises assessing clinical reasoning or problem-based learning. These latter categories exist because of the context, so tend to be less generic in their use but may also have some crossover from area to area. As we map into areas previously not explored with learning process analysis these categories will grow. Many of these categories are likely to be familiar to you. They are presented below.

Commenting:	deciding to comment, how to comment, when to comment.
Communicating:	deciding to communicate.
Concluding:	deciding to conclude.
Controlling variables:	to control variables.
Deduction:	deciding to deduce.
Extracting from experience (recalling):	deciding to recall.
Hypothesising:	deciding to hypothesise.
Investigating:	deciding to investigate, how to investigate, where to investigate.
Observing:	deciding to observe, how to observe, when to observe.
Predicting:	deciding to predict.
Questioning:	deciding to question, how to question, when to question.
Reflecting:	deciding to reflect.
Sourcing information:	deciding to source information, how to source information, when to source information.

Thinking about PBL processes: deciding to think about PBL processes.

Integrating prior
knowledge: deciding to integrate prior knowledge.

Designing an investigation: to design an investigation, how to design an investigation, where to design an investigation.

Descriptions of each category

Below are some descriptions of the more commonly encountered decisions which learners make. Some are specific to particular learning environments, such as PBL.

Category	Description
Hypothesising	The learner wanting to test a formed idea.
Questioning	The learner deciding to ask a question.
Mode of questioning	The way in which the learner decides to ask a question.
Thinking about problem-based learning (PBL) processes	The learner having an awareness of the PBL environment and adapting their learning to suit it.
Reflection/recall	Personal reflection/recall by a learner on a piece of information or a previous situation (experience).
Extracting from experience (recall)	The learner applying previously learnt knowledge to the current situation.
Sourcing information	The learner deciding to refer to a source of information, e.g. website, book, journal article.
Mode of Sourcing (how to source)	The learner accessing a source of information.
Commenting	The learner adding a piece of information to the discussion.

Mode of commenting (how to comment)	The way in which the learner decides to make a comment.
Observing	Obtaining information through sense perceptions, which can either be a passive observation of events during PBL or a decision by a participant to pay attention at any given time.

Analysing learning process maps

You may be exploring achievement of outcomes with set curriculum standards, using learning process analysis to inform your assessment of a learner, or group of learners. You might want to explore learning in a group. How learners are working, what they are getting out of it, why they are doing the things they do when they work with each other (and what they are doing). A group activity like problem-based learning, or any small group-based investigation work, are also areas where learning process analysis can help you to understand what learners are doing. You might be interested in the dynamics of the group, including how well aligned those dynamics are to the intended goals of the group. How well do my students engage in clinical reasoning? Why is a student struggling with mathematics? You can gain insight into all these aspects of learning using learning process analysis.

Learning process analysis can capture multiple aspects of learning in the same map. Take the following example:

Figure 8.10 is a learning process map from a student in a PBL session. If the goal is to look for instances of a student engaging in clinical reasoning, we have clear data about that ('Gather: new information') and why they decided to make the suggestion they did. If we are also interested in whether the student is engaging in self-directed learning, we have evidence of that as well.

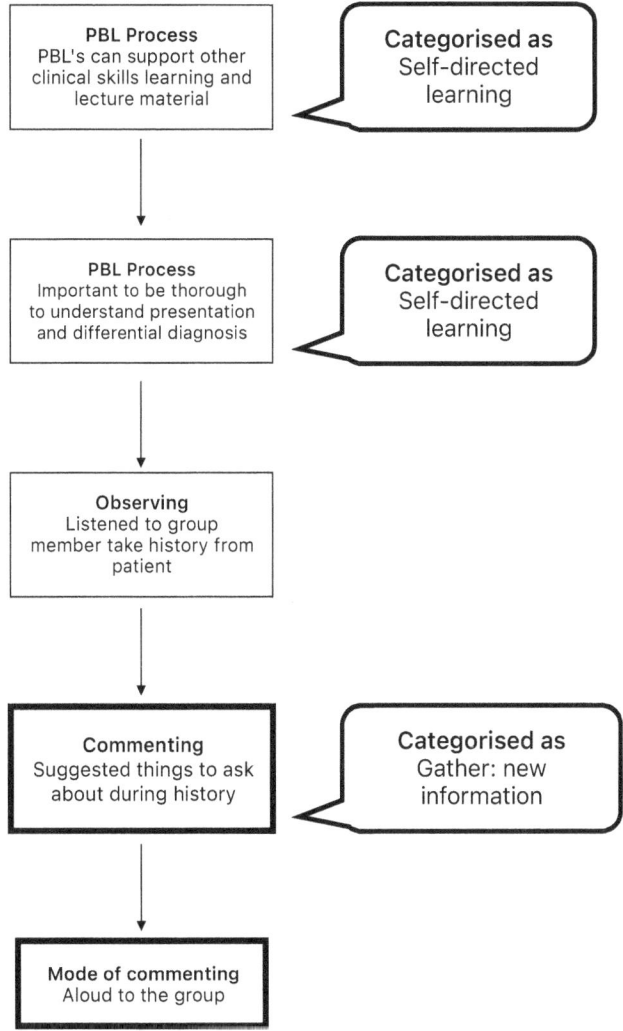

Figure 8.10: Illustrating some categories of decision-making

When analysing an individual's maps there are several features we are looking for:
1. the decisions made;
2. the decisions not made that could have been made; and
3. the reasons for decisions made.

As we have already seen, some learners decide to listen to their colleagues. Some do so for the benefit of group dynamics, others for the benefit of their learning and others for the dual benefit of group dynamics and wanting to contribute to learning, not just for themselves but also for the group.

Using learning process analysis, we can determine that learners ask questions, contribute knowledge to the group, keep the group on track, use the group to better understand lecture topics and use lecture topics as a focal point for the group's discussion.

We can determine that learners are self-regulating their learning and how so. Conversely, we can determine those who appear not to do so. We can see the nature of the creative decisions learners make when producing an artwork and why they use particular materials or features in their artwork.

We can provide unambiguous evidence that some board members ask more questions than others and why they do so and why others do not do so.

We can determine all these aspects and we can ascertain in just about all instances why people make the decisions they do. When analysing learning process maps these are the aspects we need to be looking for:

1. what decisions are made:
2. the nature of these decisions;
3. what decisions are not being made; and
4. why decisions are made.

When we analyse learning process maps systematically, we can develop a clear and accurate picture of learning. Having that clear picture provides a sound basis for feedback and from that improvement—getting better.

Analysing maps for individuals

Most assessment exercises are designed to assess individuals over time and across different content. Using learning process analysis as a method to analyse learning and how learners go about it is no different. And so, the most common way of using learning process analysis is to examine the maps of individual learners over time or across areas of learning. How this can be done depends on your goals for a particular student. You might want to track the progress of one student in one area of learning. Equally, you might want to determine how a learner approaches their learning across various areas of learning.

The key to the effective use of learning process analysis is to target specific learners for specific reasons. Let's look at one learner, E, as an example. By way of background this learner achieved well in assessments and is not confident about their knowledge. Figures 8.11 and 8.12 include learning process maps for this learner from two PBL sessions.

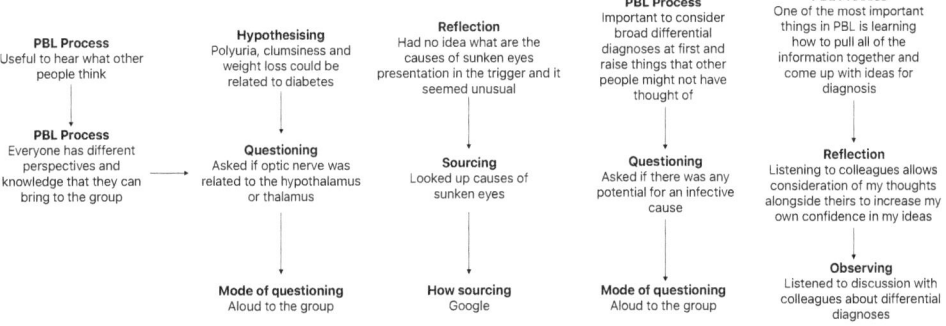

Figure 8.11: Learning process maps for learner E group session 1

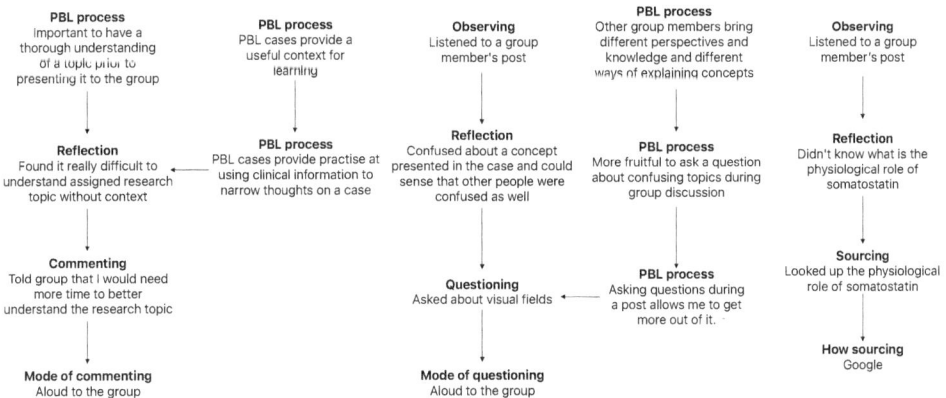

Figure 8.12: Learning process maps for learner E group session 2

From these maps we can see that learner E is:

- curious;
- prepared to ask a question to which they do not know the answer;
- prepared to open up to their colleagues about their lack of knowledge or understanding;
- aware of their lack of knowledge;
    - be prepared to do something about that
- aware of the importance of thinking broadly when engaging in clinical reasoning; and
- aware of their lack of confidence and self-directing their learning as a consequence of that awareness.

As with any measure tracking learning, using a standardised approach will help to provide confidence in your results. In practice, that means adopting a standardised approach to using a proforma, interview techniques, categorising decisions and how you present and report that information, particularly the form of your learning process maps.

Tracking the development of soft skills

Earlier in the book I showed that learning process analysis can reveal what soft skills are being used, what they look like in practice (decision-making) and how and why people are using these skills. In the learning space the most accessible and perhaps the most apt use of this capacity of learning process analysis is to track the development of soft skills for an individual learner. Particularly if we are saying that certain skills will be acquired and/or used by a learner and if we want evidence to support this acquisition.

This use of learning process analysis is particularly relevant to professional fields of study at tertiary level where employers have expectations that graduates will have acquired certain soft skills ready to use in the workplace.

Learning process analysis is a descriptive method

The learning process analysis methodology has been developed, tested and verified in a variety of research settings and a wide range of learning areas and research is ongoing. Before going any further, it is important to remember that learning process maps are designed as an analytical tool and represent descriptive data. That is, they describe what happened and why. They do not predict and are not designed to tell people prescriptively *how* to make decisions. What they are designed to do is show how people made decisions as they went about a learning task or series of tasks so that accurate and constructive feedback is available—and they can decide how to use this feedback to help them in future decisions.

Appendix 8.1: Proforma example 1

What were the main things you did during PBL?

Participant: **Date:**

PBL: [insert number and title]

Session 1		
Parts of PBL sessions	**Things I did**	
Making sense of and discussing the trigger	Asked questions?	
	Looked something up?	
	Listened to colleagues?	
	Other?	

Explanations for clinical presentation	Asked questions?	
	Looked something up?	
	Listened to colleagues?	
	Other?	
Setting research topics	Asked questions?	
	Looked something up?	
	Listened to colleagues?	
	Other?	

Session 2		
Parts of PBL sessions	**Things I did**	
Review of posts	Asked questions?	
	Looked something up?	
	Listened to colleagues?	
	Other?	
Other triggers	Asked questions?	
	Looked something up?	
	Listened to colleagues?	
	Other?	

Taking patient history	Asked questions?	
	Looked something up?	
	Listened to colleagues?	
	Other?	
Requesting investigations	Asked questions?	
	Looked something up?	
	Listened to colleagues?	
	Other?	

Diagnostic decision?	Asked questions?	
	Looked something up?	
	Listened to colleagues?	
	Other?	
Setting research topics	Asked questions?	
	Looked something up?	
	Listened to colleagues?	
	Other?	

Session 3		
Parts of PBL sessions	**Things I did**	
Review of posts	Asked questions?	
	Looked something up?	
	Listened to colleagues?	
	Other?	
Other triggers?	Asked questions?	
	Looked something up?	
	Listened to colleagues?	
	Other?	

Wrapping up problem	Asked questions?	
	Looked something up?	
	Listened to colleagues?	
	Other?	

Appendix 8.2: proforma example 2

My Art Project Diary

Things I did

Appendix 8.3: solutions to worked examples

Exercise 1

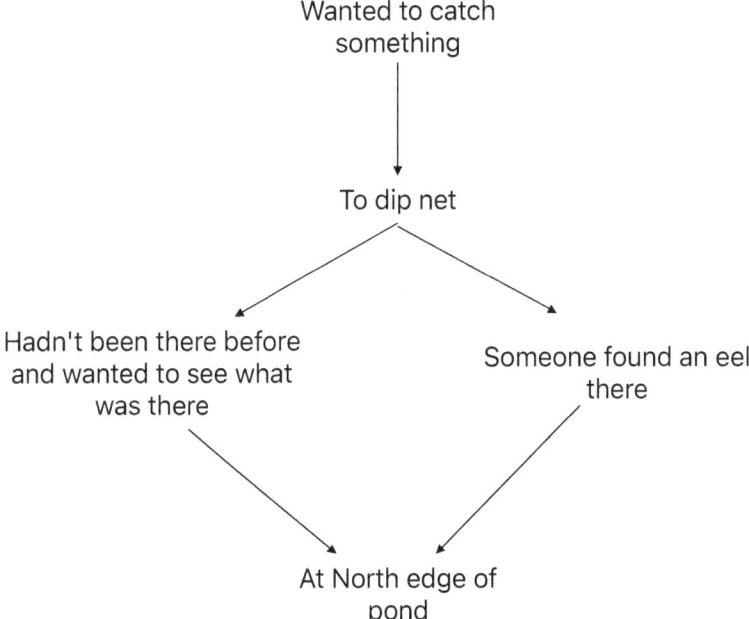

Figure 8.13: Learning process map for exercise 1

Exercise 2

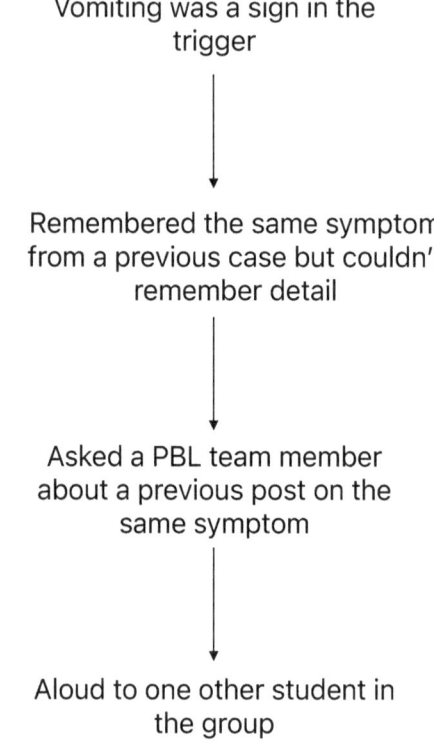

Figure 8.14: Learning process map for exercise 2

How did you find these exercises? Was there any step which caused more problems for you than others? In my experience of working with and training others to use learning process analysis, the most difficult step is the construction of the learning process map. The direction and the connections are real and it is important to be accurate with these parts of the process. Did you find categorising decisions and reasons difficult? Constructing learning process maps is a skill like any other and with practice you will get better. Please do not hesitate to contact me[30] if you want feedback or support.

---

[30] gerry.corrigan@learning52.com.au

CHAPTER NINE

Where to from here?

Learning process analysis and learning—and you and your learners

Learning occurs everywhere but it isn't always guaranteed. There are multiple reasons for this, and they will vary from learner to learner and even for the same learner as they move from one subject to another, from one type of activity to another. One of the most important reasons is that you just cannot make someone learn. As I hope I have shown so far, people consciously decide to learn and how to go about that learning in conscious and deliberate ways. Equally, some people decide to not learn in equally deliberate and conscious ways. This book is primarily, though not exclusively, written for those in the former group and those people who work with people who want to and/or are learning, and especially those who want to learn and are struggling to do so or do so inconsistently.

On a personal scale you can take the ideas and hopefully the practical approaches in this book and bring them into your learning so that you get better at learning. Alternatively, if you are working with learners, I would encourage you to bring these things into your workspace. It doesn't matter whether you are working with learners in large classes, small groups or one on one, whether those learners are young, old, or in the workplace. The same principles and foundations of LPA apply.

If you think you can improve on the LPA method please do so. If you are trying to help others learn, what I would encourage you to do is to work with a colleague or two and share approaches, successes and failures with the focus always on helping people to get better at learning. That sentiment is very much the driving force behind this book.

Deploying learning process analysis in corporate and governance scenarios

Beyond the obvious learning environments like schools, colleges and universities there are opportunities for learning in the workplace—especially those sought-after soft skills that every business wants its workers to have. As we are reminded by the business media and organisations, these soft skills are going to be increasingly important in the workplace. To first of all ascertain whether people have and or use these soft skills we need some way of detecting their use and/or measuring their use by individuals and in a range of different contexts (board meetings, group meetings). LPA can do that for us, enabling us to certify that a person has a set of skills and uses them to effect. With sufficient data, there is also the possibility of developing a soft skills index showing the degree of effectiveness of each specific soft skill for individuals. A development such as this could also be used to develop a soft skills passport for students, particularly those who are entering workplaces where soft skills are expected.

One area of extension for LPA is in corporate governance, including strategy setting, risk identification and management and planning cycles. In this environment the outcome is closer to learning about decision-making. It is still the same decision-making process of people making many micro-decisions on their way to achieving an outcome, such as when to say something, what to say, what to read, what not to read, when to ask a question—all the sorts of engagement you would expect in a governing body, along with the requisite expertise and experience that exists among a governing board's members.

In the corporate environment learning process analysis is much more closely aligned with examining decision-making of individuals who then go on to make decisions about strategy, planning cycles and risk management. As before, the benefits of learning process analysis are that it offers transparency in decision-making by making those micro-decisions, which are still deliberate and conscious ones, explicit and accessible for use in feedback for both individuals and organisations. In business, learning process analysis can facilitate identification and management of the sorts of challenges that affect larger final decisions made either by individuals, by consensus or by vote in a board setting. Having access to an individual's decision-making processes can be of significant advantage to a business's bottom line. Several examples are provided below which illustrate that assertion.

Mapping as a potential decision-making audit tool

The first example is as an auditing tool at the board level. Boards make decisions all the time, about a range of strategic options. What goes into this final decision of the board is a whole series of decision-making by every member on that board. Conducting an audit of each board member's decision-making using learning process analysis, prior to going ahead with a final decision on a key strategy or risk identification, should reveal why a board member agreed or disagreed with the decision. The board would have access to how each board member arrived at their decision, including what their reasoning was (just like in clinical reasoning or collaborating—the principle is the same), what data they accessed or chose to not access/read and any other sources of information they used to inform themselves about the topic being discussed or decided upon. You wouldn't use learning process analysis for all major decisions, as that would be counterproductive and inefficient but you might conduct 'decision audits' on an as-needs basis. You might want to target new board members, long-standing board members, particular sub-committees of a board or specific decisions like risk identification or risk appetite setting. Beyond that use, a board review, whether external or internal, might ask why some areas or people were audited and some were not—a meta-audit if you like.

Organisations are made up of individuals with different beliefs, values and interests. These differences are often the driving forces behind why decisions are made and it is these decisions, day to day, hour to hour, which impact upon the bottom line. Having reliable and accurate insight into why people make the decisions they do provides organisations with the capacity to conduct a forensic analysis of the decision-making of individuals that ultimately made the decision to agree to a proposal for a new product, as one example. An expected outcome of this approach is improved insight into collective decision-making and an improved capacity to make better decisions, more often with improved outcomes.

At this stage I want to return to those decisions mentioned above. In the first instance a manager at an organisation decides to develop a new internal human resources program for staff. She also decides to design it in such a way that staff don't just get talked to but they experience the very behaviours the program seeks to develop across the organisation.

So, what we have here are two decisions by this person. A decision to:

1. 're-design an HR program for staff'; and
2. 'design the program so the participants experience it and not have someone talk to them about it'.

Additionally, there were reasons for these decisions. For the first decision several reasons were offered by the manager. They were:

a. 'people didn't remember anything about it' (the program as it was); and
b. 'this was felt generally by others in the organisation'.

For the second decision, there were also reasons. They were because:

a. 'all the wrong messages were being sent';
b. 'I wanted to approach it differently';
c. 'behaviour is interrelated and because this program is about behaviours'; and
d. 'we didn't want any one behaviour singled out'.

These responses, provided by the manager, are the basis for learning process analysis: a decision being made and a reason, or reasons, why that decision was made. Figure 9.1 shows how this data translate into a learning process map.

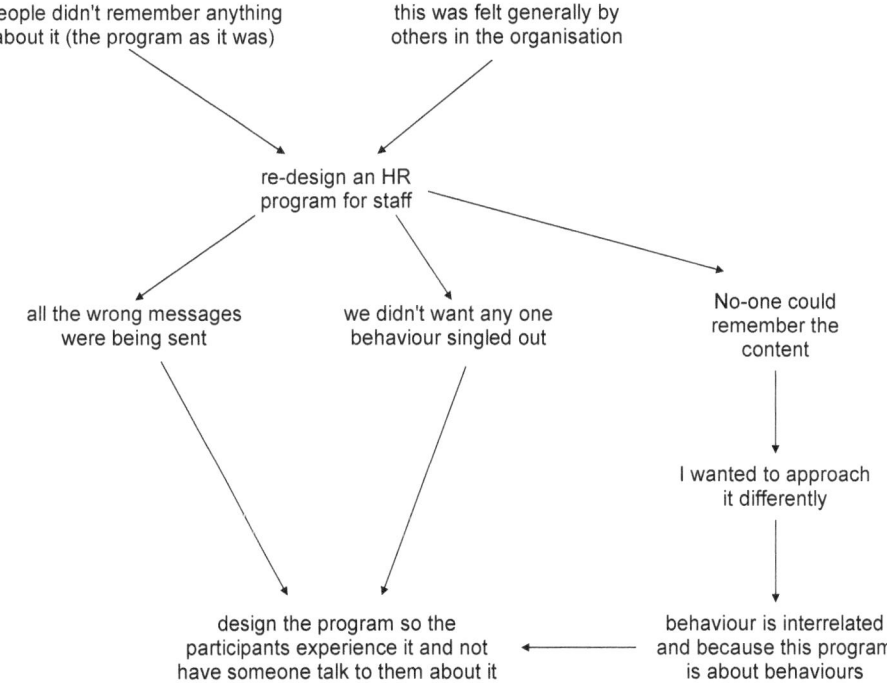

Figure 9.1: Learning process map for a manager designing a new human resources program

Diagnosing inconsistency in decision-making

Nobel laureate, Daniel Kahneman and colleagues in their book *Noise: a flaw in human judgement*[31] and in various articles in Harvard Business Review describe the concept of 'noise' (noise being different to bias). One example used to illustrate the difference between bias and noise is that of a weight scale. In this example Kahneman and colleagues ask us to think of a bathroom scale. Bias is present if the weight displayed is generally either too high or too low. If the weight displayed varies according to where you put your feet then the scale is *noisy*. Another, more visual example they use is that of a target (it could be any target, let's say it was archery). Adapted from a Harvard Business Review article is the following diagram illustrating the difference between bias and noise.

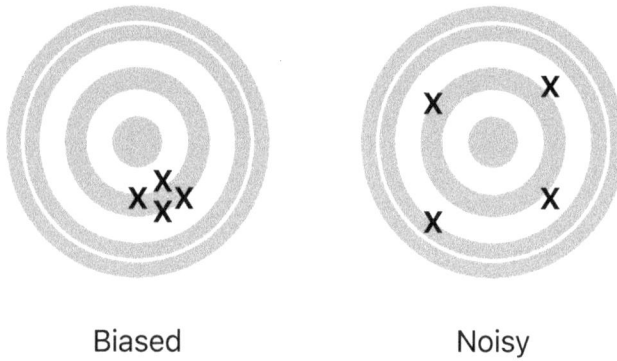

Biased   Noisy

Figure 9.2: Bias versus noise[32]

In essence noise is best described as **inconsistency in decision-making**. Kahneman and colleagues provide a convincing argument with ample evidence as to how 'noise' can have significant negative impacts upon an organisation's bottom line. To illustrate the

---

[31] Daniel Kahneman, Olivier Sibony, Cass R Sunstein 1990 Noise: a flaw in human judgement. Little, Brown Spark. New York.
[32] Adapted from Daniel Kahneman, Andrew M Rosenfield, Linnea Ghandi, and Tom Blaser, Noise: How to overcome the high, hidden cost of inconsistent decision making. Harvard Business Review. October 2016.

bottom-line impact of noise we might consider insurance quotes. And again, from one of Kahneman and colleagues' examples[33]: ideally, you do not want high variability (or noise) in insurance quotes for similar products. Various reasons include: the potential to lose business (too high a quote); the cost to the business (quote is low and accepted and ends up costing the company money); or in the example cited, the same quote request accidentally gets sent to two different offices from the same firm and comes back with wildly variable prices (a real instance)—the result was the customer going somewhere else. Much the same thing can happen in marking assessments for students. Despite the use of rubrics three different markers may well come up with different marks for the same assignment resulting in reputational damage, particularly if it happens regularly. Noise, in this instance, can cross into learning and although it may not have the million-dollar cost that it does in business, it can still present problems for both educational organisations and students.

Noise is identified via the outcome of a process whether that process be arrows hitting a target or decisions made by people. Kahneman and colleagues have suggested a noise audit as one approach to identifying and remediating noise. A noise audit is designed to determine the prevalence of noise with the overall goal of improving decision quality and so reduce noise[34].

Learning process analysis can add value to a noise audit if included as part of that process. Learning process analysis can identify the source(s) of the noise, provide detailed insight into the exact nature of the noise (i.e. a qualitative analysis) and provide clear and detailed feedback to reduce and potentially eliminate noise at the source[35]. This use of learning process analysis is one of

---

[33] See chapter 2 of Daniel Kahneman, Olivier Sibony, Cass R Sunstein 1990 Noise: a flaw in human judgement. Little, Brown Spark. New York.
[34] See Appendix A of Daniel Kahneman, Olivier Sibony, Cass R Sunstein 1990 Noise: a flaw in human judgement. Little, Brown Spark. New York.
[35] LPA can do this because noise is a product of conscious and deliberate decisions made by people.

the ways in which learning process analysis can play a role beyond the classroom.

Considerable expenditure is outlaid by organisations and individuals on accessing and adopting advice and support to overcome the challenges that affect or influence decision-making. This expenditure includes an abundance of books, tools and certified processes designed to help us make better decisions, mostly targeted at the business sector, (Six Sigma, Root Cause Analysis, Ishikawa Fish Bone Diagram and Qualitative Scenario Analysis, as some examples). Yet despite this expenditure poor decision-making both by individuals and organisations, persists. Some more memorable examples of poor decision-making are: the Challenger Space Shuttle; the 1995 failure of Barings Bank owing to lack of governance and oversight; poor decision-making, particularly around corporate governance, highlighted in the Royal Commission into the Banking, Superannuation and Financial Services Industry (Australia) and the findings of the Bergin Report into Crown Resorts (corporate governance and operations). All too often, poor decision-making is discovered in hindsight. Learning process analysis can deliver hindsight on the go.

In business, learning process analysis can facilitate identification and management of the challenges that influence decision-making. Many of these challenges are well known and include over-confidence, using incorrect data, hindsight bias, attributional bias, change blindness, cognitive biases and an over-adoption of heuristics. Learning process analysis can detect these attributes and identify if and how they are impacting upon an organisation.

Learning process analysis' capacity to reveal a person's decision-making and reasoning provides an opportunity for greater examination into and understanding of what is observed on the surface and as a consequence, greater insight into how and why people make the decisions they do. Take the manager's decision-making about the HR program in the example used earlier in this book. Insight gained from learning process analysis can be used in a number of ways in this situation. One way is to review the decision-making and reasoning before making a final decision on the proposed program. Used in this way, learning process analysis can be used as an auditing tool before a final decision is made. With the footballer's decision from earlier in the book we have insight into what might be termed a good decision. As an exemplar, her decision can be held up as the sort of decision-making required during a game. Best practice, if you will.

Learning process analysis offers a clear way to continued and sustained improvement, developing potentially more innovative individuals in organisations, efficiency in decision-making and consistently better decision-making with the overall result of significant improvement to the bottom line measured by balance sheets, tournaments/prize money/games won or better learning results for a student. Learning process analysis can be part of a market-leading approach driving individual and/or organisational improvement, resulting in an improved bottom line.

CHAPTER TEN

Learning process analysis as a research tool

There are a range of areas in which learning process analysis can be used as a research method. As described above, using learning process analysis to better understand soft skills in the workplace and how they can be used more effectively and more efficiently is one area of exploration. Some soft skills are more complex than others, certainly different anyway. There is a need to better understand the nature of learning skills in more detail, especially below the surface and how they are used effectively.

Critical thinking, the ability to obtain valid data and use it to make a final decision, is another soft skill that is complex and varies from workplace to workplace and from individual to individual. Critical thinking is crucial in any research environment. Learning process analysis offers us opportunities to gain insight into how critical thinking plays out and whether there are any identifiable patterns to how people approach and undertake critical thinking. One type of critical thinking, peculiar to specific workplaces, is clinical reasoning. Mapping provides access to the reasoning processes of individuals, whether they be medical students starting out in the process or practising professionals. Consequently, learning process analysis is an effective research method for understanding what people do, in a range of learning environments. Learning process analysis illustrates what learners do and why they do what they do—providing insights into how learners engage with clinical reasoning skills in a range of learning environments such as simulated patient sessions, objective structured clinical examinations (OSCE) or problem-based learning (PBL). The key to successful LPA is that it captures reasoning. Something that other researchers in the area of clinical reasoning acknowledged they have not captured. Through learning process analysis we can identify, at the individual level, whether learners are generating alternative hypotheses, what these are, why they are doing so and we can map this decision-making onto a taxonomy of how learners engage with clinical reasoning.

If we can continue to develop methods, such as learning process analysis and map learners' use of clinical reasoning skills onto a taxonomy, we are potentially better placed to show the extent to which individual learners have acquired various elements of clinical reasoning. We are then potentially better placed to provide learners and their teachers with accurate feedback to further assist learners' acquisition of clinical reasoning skills. Further research in this area, using learning process analysis should explore this potential.

Learning process analysis to measure governance and management

Learning process analysis is also ideally placed to be a research tool for all areas covered in this book—not just learning, although ultimately whether it is about soft skills of board decision-making, the overall outcome is learning in some form or another. Board members make decisions about strategy, the vision for an organisation, the risks that face an organisation, which risks to identify, which ones to manage and how to do so in addition to other decision-making related to corporate governance. Executives make strategic decisions in accordance with the agreed and decided-upon strategy and goals of the organisation and middle managers tend to make decisions about operational matters.

A great deal of attention is often paid to the 'agreed decision of the board'. These are the visible decisions and are readily observable (reports, minutes) and might include agreeing to a merger, or takeover offer or to develop new products. Of course, for many organisations they are required, by law, to report such things. What we do not see and what is not reported nor required to be so, is the decision-making in which a board member or director engages in both prior to and during the meeting. An example of this use of learning process analysis, initially as a research tool and eventually as an ongoing auditing tool for boards, might be for a board reviewing regular presentation of the balance sheet.

In this example the board might be reviewing the presented balance sheets, income statements, cash flow and associated explanatory notes. 'B' a board member for two years, although not an accountant, has attended a number of industry-supported training programs designed to help them understand the nature and detail of these documents. During the board meeting, 'C', an experienced director and member of the risk and audit committee and an experienced professional accountant, makes a number of observations about what is required to be added to the balance sheet and what is missing. No-one asks a question about this contribution from C, least of all B who doesn't really understand all of the points made and instead of asking for an explanation remains silent and later goes on to agree with the decisions to amend the balance sheet. A confidential exploration of B's decision-making using learning process analysis, with support from a trusted experienced director, may provide B with greater confidence to contribute to the discussion, even if it is to admit ignorance and ask a question that others might also have. Learning process analysis can assist in developing greater transparency and potentially improved governance, where matters are fully discussed and explained before a decision is made by the board.

Other examples where learning process analysis can play a role are:

- how and why some managers are more innovative than others;

- does doing an audit of board decision-making result in better outcomes;
- does examining 'noise' using learning process analysis result in a reduction of 'noise' and therefore an improvement in the bottom line; and
- Does working with beginning professional sportspeople about their decision-making enable them to be more effective, more often and consistently so with improved outcomes such as more tournaments won, more games won, higher scores for, less score against—the list is endless here.

Learning process analysis is in its infancy as a microanalytic research method. Consequently, I have tried not to overstate the implications for research of learning process analysis, whilst still wanting to describe the potential I think it offers to both research generally and also specifically, to how people learn. Theories of learning are based on data, and if learning process analysis can provide data not previously available it has the potential to inform the theoretical underpinnings of how learners learn and how people go about making decisions in every sphere of activity in which decision-making occurs.

Learning process analysis and artificial intelligence

Learning process analysis, because of its potential to reach across learning, business and sport and just about any other area where decision-making is critical, would benefit greatly by being integrated with artificial intelligence (Ai) and/or machine learning (ML) systems. Perhaps the first entry into this area would be an app which produces learning process maps from the spoken word of an individual. The diagram below captures the steps that are part of learning process analysis (A and B) and an indication where AI could play a role, including areas which might come later rather than sooner.

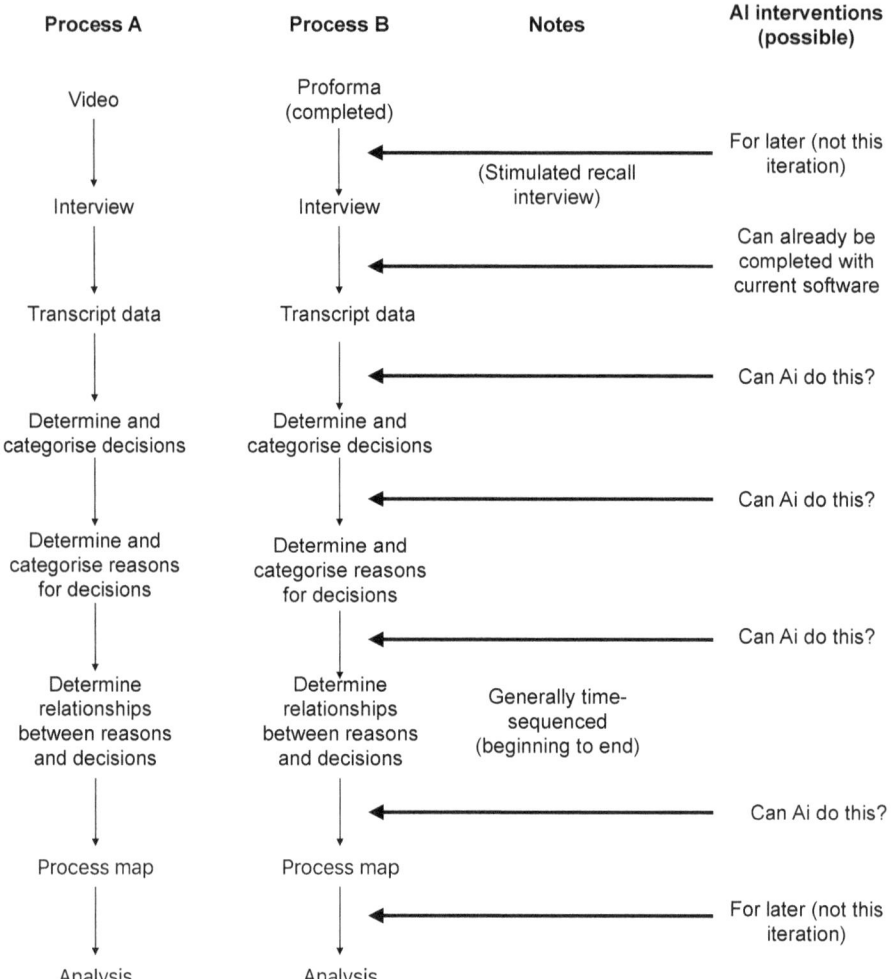

Figure 10.1: Areas where artificial intelligence could play a role in learning process analysis

Successfully integrating AI with learning process analysis (or vice versa, however it works) would enable greater reach of learning process analysis where people could employ it as they saw fit, in order to assist their learning, development, research and/ or decision-making in business. Being able to produce learning process maps more efficiently and effectively may facilitate much larger data collection sets and assist in the development of decision-making indexes. With sufficient data and appropriate indexing, it might be feasible to develop typical decision patterns people use as they go about their business, whether that be learning, sport or governance at the board level.

Future possibilities

Learning process analysis has the potential to be a contributor to the field of decision intelligence, described by Cassie Kozyrkov as a discipline that explores turning information into better actions at any scale[36]. Through our decision-making that directs our actions we navigate the world of life, learning, sport and business. Learning process analysis can play a role in revealing the nature of this decision-making. Learning process analysis can contribute to descriptive decision theory as described by Cassie Kozyrkov (CK), helping us to further understand how 'agents' (CK) make the decisions they do.

Learning process analysis may assist in moving towards artificial general intelligence (AGI). Demis Hassabis from Deep Mind has proposed artificial general intelligence as the next move for artificial intelligence. AGI is about moving to more general and capable systems of problem-solving[37]. Such systems would benefit from having an artificial intelligence system that can analyse learners' decision-making, map it out and feed these data back to the system, which may enable an improved AGI system. A form of metacognition for artificial intelligence.

We also need to consider the opportunities virtual reality (VR) technology might offer for learning process analysis and learning. Combining the potential of artificial intelligence with VR technology could make LPA available for learners, providing immediate and interactive support for the student and the educator.

---

[36] See Cassie's website to read, hear and see this aspect of decision-making first hand at https://www.kozyr.com/ accessed 17 July 2024
[37] See Deepmind.com accessed 31/8/21.

I think there are exciting possibilities and I wish you every success in your LPA journey and I am only too willing to hear your thoughts and feedback.

Gerry Corrigan at learning52.com.au